# Contents

# Introduction

Have you visited the Boundary Waters Canoe Area (BWCA), a land of lakes and pines hard on the Minnesota – Canada border?

If yes, you'll understand the tales in this book. They are real-life stories spanning decades. Reading them is like listening to a fellow canoeist in front of a crackling fire, with the wind whistling through the pines and the far-off, otherworldly cries of loons serving as background music. If you haven't visited the BWCA, these essays will give you a sense of what awaits you.

Thanks to all who submitted essays for the *BWCA Reader*, Volume 1, and special thanks to the guest authors who provided permission to reprint their inspiring words about the BWCA. This managed wilderness area is like no other place in the United States and perhaps the world. May it ever remain so.

***Barry J. Johnson***
Editor & Publisher, *BWCA Reader*
www.BWCAReader.com
BWCAReader@gmail.com

P.S. Do you have a great Boundary Waters tale?
Visit www.BWCAReader.com for more details. Your wilderness story could be published in the *BWCA Reader*, Volume 2.

# DAYS GONE BY

## The Last Canoe Trip

By guest author "Iron Mike" Hillman

*A native of Ely, Minnesota, "Iron Mike" Hillman has been an iron miner, resort manager, historical interpreter, fire fighter, radio personality, teacher, storyteller and writer. He is the author of three books, including* Stories of Old Ely and the Lake Country, *published by Singing River Publications, Inc., Copyright 2005 by Mike Hillman. This essay is reprinted with Mike's permission.*

When I came back across the Sheridan portage for my second load, he was standing at the end of the portage looking out over That Man Lake. Of all the lakes in the canoe country, my dad loved the Man chain best. We never much went past the second and smallest of the four lakes, No Man, because the fishing was so good, and the limited time he had on the weekends made getting back into This Man and the Other Man something that time and distance didn't allow. The last two lakes in the chain were saved for vacations and long weekends, so he and his partners, Joe and Johnny, spent most of their time on That Man and No Man.

The old man and his partners were part of a tradition where the canoe country was parceled up between the local men. It was an unwritten code where everybody staked out a favorite part of the country based on respect and common sense. First, it gave everybody a feeling of space and freedom that later would be called wilderness. The second thing it did was spread everyone out over the country, which made it better for the country, because it evened out the demand. I still remember the day when a canoe crossed over from Knife Lake, which lay south of the Man Chain, and my dad turned to his partner Joe and said, "Why, it's the Popishes. I wonder what the hell they are doing on our lake?" They waited until the canoe made its way over to where we were fishing, and before anyone else could say another word, Tony Popish yelled out that he was sorry to have to intrude on their space, but that it was too windy to fish on Knife Lake. The Popishes had their cousin Bernie with them, and when they said that Bernie had just been ordained a priest, Dad sort of growled an okay. But he also said not to make a habit of it. The Popishes thanked everyone for their hospitality, and then they headed toward the other end of the lake to show their respect by giving us as much space as possible.

By the time I started making regular trips with Dad and Joe in the 1960s, that system of managing the land had been in place for as long as anyone could remember, and there was no need for anyone to interfere. The people who traveled the country had a great understanding of the Quetico-Superior and, in most cases, lavished it with respect. I remember a summer evening when the fish were almost biting on a bare hook; I never wanted to stop. I wanted to keep doing it forever. Then my dad said, "Mikey, you want to come back here again don't you?" I answered that I always wanted to come back here. Then he looked over at me and said, "Mikey, if we take all the fish out of the lake tonight there won't be any point in coming back again will there? Maybe we should leave some for the next time." That was the simple lesson that was taught. You wanted to take care of the country, because you wanted to come back again.

I remember the first time we found someone had built a table and bench in one of our camps. Joe and the old man were hot about it. When I asked Dad what he was so mad about, he said that if anyone wanted to go on a picnic they should stay in a park or campground. The canoe county was no place for tables or benches.

It's hard to say when things started to change. Maybe finding the tables and chairs started it. There was a time when everything was left in camp. Open the tent doors in case any bear would come nosing around, tie the food pack up in a tree, and camp was all set for when you came back next weekend. Then one Friday evening we pulled into camp and found a note pinned to the food pack with some change left on the flat rock that made such a good cooking table. "Borrowed some sugar and powdered milk," it read, "Thanks." After that they started to break camp. Then there was the trip we came and found that someone had taken the spare canoe that was left hidden in the woods at the far end of the portage. Crime had come to the canoe country.

In order to understand the last trip my dad and I made, you have to understand the next-to-the-last trip. It was back in May of 1968, the year everything went crazy. (Ely outfitter) Bill Rom made the front cover of *Argosy* magazine where the title proclaimed him "Canoe King." You might say it helped let the cat out of the bag regarding the canoe country of Northern Minnesota. When people found out how cheap it was to rent a canoe and camping gear, that there were virtually no rules about where you could camp or how long you could stay, they descended en masse. It was Memorial Day weekend, and we were traveling with Don Berg, one of dad's friends from the mine. The trip up wasn't bad until we got to the portage going from Carp Lake to That Man, and you could see where someone had taken out a number of trees along the portage in order to make it wider. "I wonder what the hell is going on?" the old man said. It was the same with the next portage.

The answer to the riddle came on No Man's Lake when we saw two 16-foot boats pulled up along the shore of what used to be our camp, but was now in the domain of what dad referred to with scorn as "fish hogs." When we pulled close to camp you could see trout hanging all around camp, dozens of them. "Fishing looks to be pretty good," Dad said to the men who had come down to see what was up. "Yeah," one of them answered, "It's been great, and we've only just started." I remember the look on my father's face as we pulled away from that camp. It was like he had seen the thing he loved best destroyed right in front of his eyes, and you could read the hurt on his face. "I can't stay here," he said to Don Berg, "I've just got to get out of here." Don Berg shook his head and pointed the canoe back toward the portage.

When we came back for the second load the old man walked into the woods around the end of the portage, and in a short time came back carrying a set of portage wheels, which he proceeded to heave out into the lake. "Those bastards are going to have a harder time getting those boats back out than they did coming in," he said. Then he picked up the last pack and, without a backwards glance, walked down the portage. On the way back home we counted over three hundred canoes heading into the country, along with a score of boats. My father never said a word all the way back.

Dad had many chances to go back into the country. He used to tell people that the portages were getting longer and steeper and that he no longer had enough steam in his boiler to make it over the rim of the Canadian Shield. Although we never talked about it, I always knew that the reason was the things he had seen on that trip. He had seen the best of it, and now he had seen the worst of it, and he wanted to remember it the way it had always been.

In 1987 I was back running my old canoe base on Moose Lake. Dad and Mom would stop out at least once a week to say hello and to allow dad to do some fishing off the dock. One day I had to take some fishing equipment up to a party who had left it sitting on the shore of the landing, and I asked my dad if he wanted to take a ride to the Ranger Station at Prairie Portage. At first he said no, but when I pressed him by telling him that things had gotten a lot better since 1968, he reluctantly agreed. On the way up the three lake chain to Prairie Portage we passed seven canoes with our tow boat, and the old man told me that this was more like it. When we got to the portage, we were informed by the ranger that the head of the Quetico Park was paying a visit, and we had best make sure that everything was in order. By a twist of fate, the head of the park ended up being an old friend of my father's whom dad had met when Don Money was a young ranger back in the 1950s. They had a wonderful visit talking about the old days and the way things used to be. On the way back, he turned to me and said that maybe they had turned things around and that he'd like to see more of it.

That next spring, Dad and I took our final trip to No Man's Lake. The trees of our old camp had filled back in, and we fell asleep at night listening to the sound of the river heading north. It was like being home again, and was a wonderful trip. Everyone caught fish, except Dad, but he didn't seem to care; he was past that point in his life. The thing that pleased him the most was that the entire trip all we saw of humanity were two canoes that passed through our near-perfect wilderness, like a mirage, and were gone.

Dad was standing at the end of the portage when I came up to him and asked him if he was coming, or if he planned to go home with someone else. "I want to thank you for bringing me back here," he said. "This is the last time I'm ever going to see this lake and I wanted to thank you for the gift." "Don't be going soft and mushy on me," I said. "No," he answered, "It's just that I'm no damned good anymore, got no sense of balance, can't carry a pack anymore, it's time for me to call it quits. This is a place for young people and not for old farts like me. But I want to thank you for giving me back something I'd lost. This is the way it was before, and this is the way it should always be, and now, thanks to this trip, it's way I will always remember it."

Then he turned back to the lake. I picked up the last pack and headed toward Sheridan Lake and the way back home. Whenever I think of my father, he is standing at the end of that portage, looking east into the rising sun of a new morning, shining down on the place he loved the best.

## *Post-World War II Honeymoon in the Pre-BWCA Wilderness*
By Marge Jergenson

"You're going WHERE on your honeymoon!?" friends asked following our July, 1947 wedding.

It was hot in Minneapolis, 95 degrees, and I answered eagerly, "We're going north to the Gunflint Trail on a really cool canoe trip from Gunflint Lodge to Saganaga." My new husband and I were both novice canoeists, eager to escape the heat and explore the untamed wilderness.

I traded my wedding dress for jeans and we were on our way. Our 10-day food supply was heavy. We carried Val-Packs, (Army surplus backpacks that sold cheap after World War II). They were stuffed with various cans (which were not prohibited at the time) oatmeal, powdered milk, bacon, eggs, pancake mix that needed only water, canned pork and beans, jams/jellies, and dried apricots.

The Gunflint Trail at that time was not paved. We endured a slow, dusty but enjoyable drive and the sight of a moose crossing the road, as well as a gaunt grey wolf. Arriving at the lodge, we were welcomed by Justine Kerfoot and her son, Bruce. They briefed us on our proposed route, which included multiple portages. We set off by canoe, with the U.S. on "our side," and Canada across "the pond." We saw no one, made our portages, and chose lovely rocky sites to put in and rest. The loons called, the moon lighted our path, and we were mesmerized by the beauty of the wild as we camped. The next day my husband had the bright idea of testing the "tip-ability" of our canoe. Knowing that I could not swim, while he was an excellent swimmer, he left me and the canned goods on shore when he tried to tip our canoe. He succeeded. As he floundered around the cold water, I knew he was able to swim to shore (hopefully with the canoe in tow) so I proved to be a thoughtful bride sitting on the rocky shore, saying, "I can't save you so I will photograph you proving what a macho man you are." Unfortunately, those classic pictures have disappeared.

We were truly alone on our honeymoon. We did spot one bear swimming across our path and entering the campsite we were headed toward. We had no choice but to follow him, fearlessly. Countless playful chipmunks entertained us when we camped, convinced that we had brought "treats." As we paddled our way through the most beautiful chain of lakes imaginable, we knew that this, our precious honeymoon, was totally unforgettable.

Six months later, we were on our way to Africa as missionaries, but our Boundary Waters honeymoon memories remain forever in our hearts. My love of camping and enjoying the wilderness prepared me for many experiences in Cameroun (now the Republic of Cameroon). My husband lived to be 94 and I am now 90 years old, treasuring still God's gift of the Boundary Waters. Justine is gone, Bruce Kerfoot is an adult managing his mother's dream, and all are welcome to come and experience the joy of paddling and the cry of the loon.

# The Summer Of BWCA Love
By Bill Holden

The summer of 1967 was the height of hippie power, peace, love and happiness. Summer love is often fleeting, but that August four youths from Minneapolis canoed into the beginning of a lifelong relationship. Our 14-day journey through more than 40 BWCA and Quetico lakes sparked a love affair with the wilderness that burns to this day

We had heard of the concept of portaging and our teenage minds developed a wonderful idea. It made no sense to empty a canoe of its weighty gear when four strapping young men were capable of astounding feats of physicality. We would leave the gear inside and carry the canoe, two guys to a side, then paddle on.

Somehow we made it across that first portage and only dropped the canoe four times, twice onto rocks. We quickly discovered that chewing gum and Band-Aids repair holes punched into an aluminum canoe. We returned to our second canoe and emptied it of gear. Our second portage was more efficient, though we made a note to include canoe portage pads on future trips.

We grossly miscalculated the demands that four mountainous appetites would have on our food pack. It was not of much concern early in our trip, since we caught walleye, bass, and northern pike on most lakes. The fish were always "better than eating candy." Later, we met three other voyageurs on a portage and shared our precious cans of beef stew, beans, and chicken. As a result, our entire last day's ration (per person) was a morning cup of oatmeal, a lunch drink of Kool-Aid and a supper cup of Lipton's onion soup. We started to know hunger.

Our last night's camp was canoe-country perfect. It was on a large island. I set out to explore and spotted a chattering little red squirrel on a nearby log. Almost instinctively I threw a rock at the impish rodent and landed a direct hit. I felt sorry for the warm bundle of red fur in my hand. There's not much meat on a red squirrel, but each ravenous voyageur got a few bits in his cup of soup and it was good.

As a seagull soared overhead, I tossed the handful of bloody rodent guts offshore. The gull eyed the morsel but then a whirlpool slurp of epic proportions drew the guts into the dark depths. A huge fish had stolen the gull's supper.

I retrieved my spinning rod, tied on a black Hula Popper and cast to the spot. The lure bobbed on the surface for 10 seconds and then disappeared in a maelstrom. The fish in Hemingway's little book was bigger but the epic battle on that granite island point was just as dramatic. The fish fought with reel-grinding power. When it launched its bronzed, head-shaking body into the air, we gasped in awe. It was the biggest slab of a small-mouth bass we had ever seen. In time, I landed the beast. I slid the trophy up on the rocks then displayed him to the celebratory hoots of joy from my audience. This was the fish of a lifetime. My brother had already pulled the skillet and fillet knife out of the empty food pack. I informed my fellow voyageurs that "no way were we eating this fish." Out-voted three to one, I prepared the fish for our dinner. I actually portaged out the remains and had a taxidermist work his magic. That relic from our baptismal trip to the BWCA – estimated at six pounds – still hangs on my father's wall.

One other memory from that long-ago trip stands out.

A day after catching the big fish, we spotted another canoe. We noticed there were three expertly synchronized paddlers propelling the canoe like an arrow toward the same portage we were headed for. We had not seen any other guys for three days, and were interested to meet the fellow voyageurs and discuss lakes explored, fish caught, and routes to follow.

As we closed the distance to the other canoe, the realization hit us simultaneously; the three paddlers were … girls! Very pretty girls. They were co-eds from California heading home from a month-long canoe trip three times the length of journey we were on. Plus, we would be following the same route the next day! Quite a bonus for young men in the wilderness.

The stories from that long ago canoe trip were just the first links on our priceless chain of wilderness memories.

# Boundary Waters Everywhere

By Rick Gold

Decades ago, fresh out of high school, a friend and I decided to paddle into the Quetico, the Canadian counterpart of the BWCA.

We deemed ourselves ready for the less well-traveled Quetico because of two previous guided trips into the BWCA with our high school Wilderness Training class. Another friend working a stint at Camp Widjiwagan on Burntside Lake, outside Ely, Minn., offered to outfit our expedition with loaned gear.

We pooled our meager resources, enough to amass a few jerry tubes of peanut butter, some Bisquick, and a big bag of trail mix. We would supplement our meals with the many fish we expected to catch on our 10-day trip. We'd drink water from the lakes.

We set out from Widji with the canoe, tent, sleeping bags, axe, and compass on loan from our outfitter friend. Putting in at the Moose Lake portage, we enjoyed a glorious day that saw us paddle enthusiastically to Crooked Lake on the U.S.-Canada border where we camped our first night.

The next morning after our Bisquick pancakes with wild blueberries cooked over our small campfire, we headed north to Argo Lake just inside the Quetico Provincial Park of Canada.

The wind picked up that day and we secured a campsite on Darkey Lake. That second night of our trip the rain began; it continued raining for the remainder of our journey.

The unrelenting rain made the Quetico resemble one big flooded basin. Overflowing rivers and flooding lakes made our maps difficult to read. Thankfully, we had a compass and were confident we could locate the wooden posts that marked portages in the Quetico, and thus navigate our way out of Canada.

Then we lost the compass.

When the canoe capsized in one of the raging rivers (previously a quiet, meandering steam) my sleeping bag went in and was rendered a waterlogged burden. I eventually tossed it aside. The axe and compass disappeared beneath the water, as did our trail mix and Bisquick.

You would think a tent in its storage sack might float. Not so.

We scrambled to the stream bank (or more precisely, the shallower water overflowing the bank) to gather ourselves, recover any gear we could and ... and then what?

Somehow, we'd hung on to the canoe and paddles. Two tubes of peanut butter were saved. We had one sleeping bag, and a lighter. That was it, save the soaking wet clothes on our backs.

Looking around, we spotted a structure! Shelter from the rain! It was an old garage-type building. Its gravel floor was soaked with diesel fuel. A decrepit oil burner sat in one corner. We tried in vain to light it. No oil. No dry kindling to start a fire. I'd have burned cash if we had had any.

A Cessna appeared high overhead. We waved our arms and paddles hoping to be seen. The plane flew on.

At least we were out of the rain as night fell. We hunkered down in the smelly garage, trying to make a bed of the one wet sleeping bag we had. It was a cold, uncomfortable, sleepless night.

I had my last squeeze of peanut butter the next morning and we headed out in search of the long portage that would lead us out of the Quetico and back to Moose Lake in the BWCA.

We spent two days paddling back and forth in the continuous rain peering into the flooded bays and inlets trying to spot that solitary pole that marked the portage out.

I had long since become nauseated by the smell of the peanut butter my bow-man kept eating. I instead dreamed of a hamburger, onion rings, and chocolate malt from Porky's, a now-defunct fast food joint in St. Paul. I mentally repeated those three menu items over and over in a silent, rhythmic chant. It kept me going.

Early on day three of our meandering paddling, I focused on an area I had already looked at multiple times. Suddenly I spotted the post marking the portage. Eureka! We were saved!

We surprised our friend/outfitter by coming out of the wilderness three days earlier than planned.

He was not happy that we'd lost most of his gear. Nor was he terribly impressed with our ordeal. I don't believe we had to pay for those lost items, but we would have been glad to work off the expense at the camp doing chores. None were assigned.

All the way back to St. Paul I continued my hamburger, onion rings, and chocolate malt chant until I pulled into the drive-thru at Porky's and ordered my fantasy meal.

I haven't been back to the BWCA since, but used the knowledge of what not to do in the wilderness on my subsequent employment with the National Park Service in the backcountry of Alaska.

Valuable experience indeed.

# Two Captains, Two Explorers
By David Arbeit

At age 50 when I moved to Minnesota in 1994, I was ignorant about anything related to canoe camping, let alone the Boundary Waters Canoe Area. Having grown up in New York, I was a city kid totally out of his element in nature. Fast forward to now, and almost any time between ice-out and early fall you're likely to find me in the BWCA with my life-mate Susan, paddling solo canoes so small that you might worry about our mental condition.

Shortly after arriving in Minnesota, Susan visited John, her avid canoeist brother in Buffalo, New York. She took a paddle in his 10-foot, 17-pound Adirondack pack canoe. When she returned home, she announced that we needed to get our own little canoes and that John was coming to visit; he had always wanted to paddle in the BWCA. I scrambled for a map and discovered that it covered a huge part of the state. If I was to become a Minnesotan, I needed to paddle a canoe. Buying a stable tandem seemed more sensible than tiny solo canoes, even for short excursions on local lakes. But Susan had paddled John's little canoe; the die had been cast.

We ended up buying two boats made by Peter Hornbeck, who had been building Kevlar adaptations of small solo canoes designed and made by J. Henry Rushton for naturalist George Washington Sears in the 1880s. Known as Nessmuk, Sears was a petite man who wanted to explore the Adirondacks without hiring a guide to paddle the heavy guide boats used during that era. He wrote about his travels in the tiny 10-foot Wee Lassie and 9-foot Sairy Gamp in *Forest and Stream* magazine. These classics now are on display in the Adirondack Museum. Hornbeck's adaptations, made of modern materials, are – like the originals – paddled with a long double paddle, much like kayaks. The two boats Peter shipped to Minnesota weighed less than 30 pounds together. Nested when they arrived, the shipping agent thought one of the two canoes had been lost until we opened the well-wrapped package.

That summer of 1995, our new little canoes and John's decade-old 12-foot Hornbeck arrived in Ely for the first of many Boundary Waters visits. They made an immediate impression.

As I parked the car by Piragis Outfitters with our all three of our canoes on my double rack, an excited fellow rushed over to greet us: "Are those Hornbecks? I've heard about them but have never seen any up here."

The canoes proved to be comfortable in northern lakes. They have since taken us on almost two dozen trips covering more than 2,000 miles of BWCA waters. They've traveled gracefully across glassy lakes and bobbed over waves on lakes decorated with frightening white caps, taking on nary a drop of water. They've been to remote spots along the Canadian border where we saw no other people for several days. They've prompted curious looks from fellow travelers we've met at portages and astonishment from those who hefted these featherweights. And, though unusually small, they've gracefully carried our well-chosen gear for trips lasting as long as two weeks.

This "city boy" has aged quite a bit since that first visit to the Boundary Waters, but he still looks forward to that time of year when the ice is out and the black flies have not yet emerged. That's the time when he and Susan pack up their gear, fasten their Hornbecks to the canoe rack that never leaves their car, and head north for the first wilderness experience of the year. Buying a tandem canoe back in the beginning might have been a good choice, but going "solo together" has suited us just fine. In our two boats, we're two captains and two explorers.

## *The Unpopular Habit of Max the Dog*
By Roxanne Chmielewski

Forty years ago, when I was in my early 20s, the highlight of my summers was an annual canoe trip to the BWCA with a rotating cast of good friends. My one constant companion on these adventures was my best friend, Max, half-Labrador Retriever and half-Standard Poodle. This was long before Labradoodles were popular; Max was just a mutt. He was coal black, weighed 110 pounds, was smart and well-mannered, and went with me everywhere.

Max's only significant fault was a sensitive stomach. He would (and did) eat anything he encountered. If it was not normal dog or people food, however, it quickly left him from one end or the other.

He loved riding in vehicles, including boats and canoes. He would sit motionless watching the world go by, a big doggy grin on his face. For some unknown reason the motion of canoes did not agree with Max's sensitive stomach. He would gladly climb into the canoe and settle himself comfortably on the bottom out of the way of the paddlers. Good dog. But then, without fail, after about 30 minutes and with no warning, he would upchuck into the bottom of the canoe. My companions never appreciated this little trick. There would be yelling and swearing and gagging. I would clean up the mess, and we would continue on our way. Max was very faithful in this habit; no matter what or when he ate or how calm or wavy the water, he always did his trick. You could rely on that dog. I tried to anticipate when it was coming so I could direct his head over the side of the canoe, but he was always too quick.

I am grateful my companions allowed Max and I to join them each year, despite that obnoxious habit. I hope my grandchildren and their children will be able to enjoy the BWCA, hopefully without a canoe-barfing dog!

## Canoeing pre-BWCA: The First-Visit
By Donald Marpe

Our family became acquainted with the canoe country one rainy day in 1947 when my wife Ellen and I – newlyweds on our honeymoon – hiked the Echo Trail. This so called "trail" was hardly more than a 60-mile "two track" which bisected the massive wilderness area northwest of Ely. In 1978, that area would eventually become the western part of the BWCA.

Our exploration showed us several nice spots for overnight camping and a number of trails appeared to be access points to more wilderness, if one had a canoe. Neither of us had any significant canoe experience but our interest was awakened.

We spent the winter assembling gear. By the second summer of our married life (1948) we felt we were well-prepared for a canoe trip. We had previously hiked in over the canoe portages to the Nina-Moose River and to the Little Indian Sioux River. We saw on our maps that these two rivers each flowed into the same long chain of lakes and portages, including two large bodies of water, Lac La Croix and Loon Lake. Conceivably, a canoe put in at one river could be taken out out at the other, although it was 65 miles from put-in to take-out. After securing a canoe from an Ely outfitter, we headed up the Echo Trail to the portage accessing the Nina-Moose River. We figured there'd be no problem traveling the distance in one week as long as we had enough to eat.

Our first realization that the trip might not be as relaxing as we'd envisioned came when we unloaded the car and began portaging gear down to the Nina-Moose River. We didn't yet know about Duluth packs. Our loose stuff was put into a sea bag which I'd retained from my military service. After four trips each we got everything to the overflowing canoe; there was just enough room for Ellen, me and our paddles.

During those years there was no ban on cans or bottles in canoe country so that's what we had (we didn't yet know about dehydrated trail packs and freeze-dried food). We called our large rubberized food sack "forty acres" because of how wide it spread out on the ground. I could barely lift it. Our tent was almost as heavy. Right from the start it appeared each portage was going to require four trips, but after the second day we somehow managed to reduce this number to three. (In later years we usually got across a portage in two trips, and one year, on a visit to Lake Polly from the Kawishiwi entrance to the BWCA, Ellen and I managed to make all the portages in one trip.)

When we pushed the canoe into the Nina-Moose River it was gratifying that we still had some freeboard and that the river was deep enough to float us. When we went around that first bend and had only wilderness in front of us, we imagined the trip would be great and wonderful. By the time we got up to Nina-Moose Lake and made our first camp, we'd gained some experience, including having a red squirrel chew his way into the sea bag. We we were dog tired.

Our first canoe trip was in mid-June and neither one of us knew the difference between a black fly and a blue fly. This is mosquito season in the canoe country, but I don't recall that we really cared about the bugs. Possibly it was our enthusiasm that kept us paddling in and our desperation that got us out, or maybe the bugs just weren't as bad then as they've been in other years. We fished a lot, caught enough walleyes to eat, and we paddled a lot, since 65 miles is a bit of a distance. Sadly (in hindsight), we also added to the pile of cans and bottles that we found back in the brush at each campsite.

When camping on 25 Island in Lac La Croix our third night in, the weather turned bad so we were forced to stay in camp for a second night. The next day the wind died down a bit and we managed to successfully launch the canoe without being swamped. We had a wild ride across a large stretch of open water, finally reaching 41 Island where we planned to spend the night. As we unloaded the canoe we realized that we'd sat on our life jackets for the wild trip across that open stretch of big water. Lucky and dumb!

The country seemed to be deserted but at the far east end of Lac La Croix we were overtaken by a Native American who was piloting a rowboat with a small outboard and towing a string of five or six similar rowboats. With hardly a look or a wave, he soon disappeared between islands. We surmised that he was headed to one of the resorts, or maybe up into Canada. We never saw or heard him again, nor did we ever see any of the boats he was towing. Further west, during our sixth day, we caught up with two teenage boys in another canoe, the first paddlers we'd seen since we began our trip. They were very bug bitten, looked totally disorganized and didn't seem to have any packs for their gear. Their food supply consisted of about a half peck of potatoes rolling round loose in the bottom of the canoe. One of the boys had a pistol in a holster strapped to his side, which he said was their bear protection. They told us how anxious they were to get back to civilization and Chicago. Their anxiety didn't translate to power at the paddle, though, since Ellen and I easily beat them to Beatty Portage, which is the mechanical lift used to get over the portage into Loon Lake.

Near the end of the trip, while trying to find the first portage out of Loon Lake into the Little Indian Sioux River, a Forest Service plane circled us several times. We didn't know why so went on our way after we found the portage (it's still probably marked wrong on the canoe country maps). At the Devil's Cascade portage was a fire tower and a Forest Service cabin (both have since been removed). We could hear talking and laughing in the cabin, and soon three college-age guys came out. They were a portage-clearing crew and were getting ready to hike out the next day since their week, and their work at this area, was completed. They had the keys to the fire tower so invited us to climb up with them. It was a great view and gave us a good perspective of just how far we'd gone on this canoe trip. Later that afternoon we crossed the last portage and reached the parking area which was connected by a two-track road to the Echo Trail. Our car, of course, was still up at the Nina-Moose River parking lot. We calculated that to be about six miles back up the Echo Trail.

We had hardly walked a half-mile before a Forest Service pickup truck stopped and gave us a ride. This Forest Service Ranger had a lot of questions. When we explained where we'd come from he asked if we'd seen a portage cutting crew on the trails. It turned out he'd been searching for them and had been flying the plane that circled us earlier in the day. We didn't tell him that his crew had been taking it easy in the cabin while he was flying around.

Ellen and I have paddled and camped throughout this area all during its transition from raw wilderness – with few rules or restrictions – to the finely regulated BWCA. Our experiences led to many family members becoming acquainted with the BWCA. This includes not only our own children, but even our two dads, who each made several trips, and our two mothers, who at least saw this country from the near edges, and most of our siblings. No wonder it finally got so crowded that you needed a permit.

## Youth Conservation Corp: Beginning a Life of Travels by Canoe
By Jeffrey Sheehan

When I was 16 years old, my mother found something for me to do that summer. It was the YCC - Youth Conservation Corp. When she was a kid, she said, men who couldn't find work were employed by the government to build roads, bridges and more.

The State of Minnesota was starting this again in northern Minnesota, in the BWCA.

I was a city kid, newly relocated to the country. My summers consisted of playing baseball with friends every day at the park, without parents. I had just gotten my first job, a real job paying $3.65 per hour!

My mother asked me if I would be interested in applying for YCC, and I said, "Sure, I guess." That changed my life forever. I traveled to Isabella to the Environmental Learning Center (ELC) just up the road from the Knotted Pine Bar on Flat Horn Lake. We were to live in barracks with 50 other 16- to 18-year-old kids from all over Minnesota.

Our job from June through August was to work with the Minnesota Department of Natural Resources and the Fish & Wildlife and Forestry Departments. Our pay was $3.75 per hour, minus room and board, but we would receive a high school credit. Working in the woods of the BWCA, we needed steel toed-boots, heavy-duty pants, hard hats, gloves and eye protection. Our jobs included building trails, clearing brush, building or updating campsites, or whatever else the government agencies could think of to keep us busy.

Each group left the ELC on Monday morning, travelled to their worksite, then set up camp (two tents and provisions for eight people – four boys and four girls). We had just enough food to make it through the week. No more, no less.

One of my many work assignments was to canoe up Perent Lake to rebuild some campsites and put in new latrines. We had four canoes loaded with supplies, plus two latrine kits, travelling down a river to the lake. Since the river was shallow at times, and blocked by beaver dams at other times, we had to get out and drag the canoes as the bugs attacked. Upon reaching the lake, the breeze finally kept those huge Minnesota mosquitos at bay.

We set up camp on an island and started our week of living in the woods. What could have been better for a bunch of 16-year-old kids?

One day as we canoed to work, our work leader saw a smoldering fire at a camp site. We canoed over to find a fire sputtering in the moss and vegetation debris around the fire ring. Our work leader was about to put it out, but we sprang into action. Using our metal helmets, we hauled water from the lake and doused the smoldering fire. The best part about this was that our work leader was on the Forestry Fire Crew and told us that he was going to put our crew in for "fire duty" pay.

During this summer of exploring and working in the woods, we had the chance to see some of the prettiest lakes in Minnesota: Dumbbell Lake, Snowbank Lake, the Sawbill Trail and its lake, Elbow Lake, Ima Lake and Hatch Lake nearby, Nine Mile Lake and Bald Eagle Lake. We visited Gooseberry Falls and swam in the Temperance River; we looked for agates on the shores of Lake Superior.

That summer working with the YCC was a chance of a lifetime. We learned that we could work together, we could move logs that seemed too big, we could fit eight people, gear and food into a 12-passenger van and live out of it for a week, and we found out that the outdoors was pretty neat.

For this bunch of kids from the cities and farm country, that summer was the beginning of a life of travels by canoe, by foot, and in tents, into the woods, lakes and streams of the BWCA.

## Introducing the BWCA to Generations of Paddlers

By Lynn Huemann (Submitted by Elden Huemann)

My Boundary Waters adventures began after a trip on the Gunflint Trail in 1979. I'd read about the trail in magazines, and I knew I had to visit.

Rockwood Lodge was the place I chose. I made reservations for myself and my spouse. It was a good choice. We enjoyed our stay then, and many times after. We spent time canoeing on Poplar Lake and took day trips into the BWCA. We never camped – my wife wasn't too fond of that idea – but I knew in the back of my mind that one day I would.

My first overnight paddle trip was in 1983. I chaperoned a church youth group. I did this again two years later. Both trips started on Seagull Lake. A guide was furnished and we covered a lot of area in only five days. A LOT of portages, camp set-ups and take-downs! Alpine, Jasper, Eddy, Knife and Hanson Lakes ... and many more! It was a rewarding experience for me, and wilderness living was a great experience for these young people (ages 15-16). They had a good feeling about all that they had accomplished: carrying canoes and packs, paddling, and all of the camping duties. They had to get along without the usual "every-day needs" of phones, toilets and showers, and fast food!

I was now determined that my family had to be introduced to the BWCA. This included my four children, their spouses, and eventually my eight grandchildren. Our first family trip was in 1987. It included my sons-in-law, Maynard and Stuart, and a close friend of theirs. We traveled from Rockwood Lodge and set up camp on Crossbow Lake. We took day trips from there and caught enough walleye and smallmouth bass for all of our evening meals. It doesn't get any better than that! Two trips followed in 1988 and 1990. My son Brian joined us in 1990.

Two portages that were quite challenging for me were the Meeds Lake portage out of Poplar and the portage between Vista and Misqua. The first was a mile long and the second quite rocky. The effort was worth it! Outstanding scenery! Stairway portage included beautiful waterfalls. I paddled many lakes over the years, from Poplar to Horseshoe to Duncan ... and many more.

Now it was time to include the grandkids. Many years and trips later I have accomplished that goal. All eight of them have camped with "Pappa" in the BWCA. I now have great-grand-children coming into my life and I would like to think that they will get the opportunity to enjoy our precious BWCA.

This wilderness area offers freedom and expansive solitude, challenge and personal integration with nature. The awesome sight of canoeing around a bend and seeing a majestic Bull Moose is difficult to describe. The call of a loon from across the lake at night, or hearing a wolf howling in the distance, is amazing. On one occasion a bear walked right into our campsite as we were cooking!

I have made 14 trips into the BWCA. Last summer, a couple of the grandkids told me, "Pappa, we need to make another BWCA trip next summer." I am 78 years old now. I am not sure this is a good idea or not. Still, I applied for a permit for late July and we will see what happens.

> *"Now I see the secret of the making of the best persons. It is to grow in the open air, and to eat and sleep with the earth."* – Walt Whitman

# BWCA QUIZ #1

**1.)** How long is the Gunflint Trail?

**2.)** What is a "Derecho" (pronounced "de-RAY-cho") and why is it notable for the Boundary Waters Canoe Area?

**3.)** What happened on March 27, 1949, at the home of Ely canoe outfitter William "Bill" Rom?

**4.)** What is the passenger / weight limit for the classic Quetico 17, the 17-foot aluminum canoe from Alumacraft?

**5.)** What causes giardiasis, with symptoms of diarrhea, flatulence, stomach / abdominal cramps, nausea and dehydration?

**BWCA Quiz #1 – Answers**

1.) The trail runs 57 miles from Grand Marias to Saganaga Lake.

2.) A "Derecho" is a large, long-lasting straight-line windstorm. On July 4 and 5, 1999, a huge derecho caused a massive timber blowdown in the BWCA.

3.) A homemade bomb exploded next to his house. The explosive was presumably built and planted by someone angered by Rom's support of restrictions against motorized boat and plane travel into what is now the BWCA . Luckily, no one was killed or injured, and damage was minimal. No one was ever arrested for the crime.

4.) The Quetico 17 by Alumacraft is rated to carry up to four passengers or 750 total pounds (passengers plus gear).

5.) Giardiasis is caused by giardia, a microscopic parasite that lives in the intestines of animals (and people). Giardiasis can be contracted in the BWCA via unfiltered water from lakes, stream, or ponds.

# FISH TALES

## *The Great Boundary Waters Fish*
By guest author Tom Dickson

*These excerpts are reprinted with permission from Tom Dickson, author of* The Great Minnesota Fish Book, *illustrated by Joseph R. Tomelleri, published by the University of Minnesota Press, copyright 2008. Dickson grew up fishing in Minnesota. He now lives in Montana and is the editor of* Montana Outdoors.

### WALLEYE
*Sander virtreus*

Minnesota's beloved state fish is North America's largest member of the perch family, making it a cousin of the sauger, yellow perch and darters. The fish is named for its eyes, which appear clouded or glassy in sunlight due to a reflective layer of pigment behind the retina called the tapetum lucidum. Similar to that in a cat's eye, this ocular feature allows the retina to absorb extra light, providing the walleye with excellent vision in dark or muddy water. The "wall" in the common name derives from the Icelandic word vagl, meaning "film over eye."

Walleyes feed primarily at night or in low light, when they can see well but prey such as perch cannot. On sunny days, walleye head to water up to 40 feet deep to escape the light. But when the wind kicks up into what anglers call a "walleye chop," surface waves refract the sun's rays and the fish can move to shallow water where there is more prey – and where anglers have an easier time catching them. On cloudy days with a slight wind, walleyes may be in shallow water all day.

STATE RECORD: 17 pounds, 8 ounces, Seagull River (Cook County), 1979

## SMALLMOUTH BASS
*Micropterus dolomieu*

The eighteenth-century voyageurs who paddled the lakes and rivers along today's Minnesota-Ontario border never encountered a single smallmouth bass. That fact may surprise those who today consider this hard-fighting fish to be as integral to canoe country as loons and Duluth packs. Yet in Minnesota, smallmouth are native only to the Mississippi River and its tributaries. Stocking by the federal government in the early 1900s, an accidental introduction to the Rainy River around the same time, bait-bucket introductions by anglers in the mid-1900s, and more recent plantings by the (Minnesota) Department of Natural Resources (DNR) have created self-sustaining populations throughout the state.

Early French explorers who came to North America called the newly discovered species "the fish that struggles."

STATE RECORD: 8 pounds, West Battle Lake (Otter Tail County), 1948

## LAKE TROUT
*Salvelinus namaycush*

The lake trout is a legendary fish of the North Country, reaching large sizes in Lake Superior and canoe country waters. In lakes with fatty forage fish such as ciscoes, lakers occasionally reach 30 pounds.

Lake trout are voracious predators and have been found with fish half their body length in their stomach.

On inland lakes, most lake trout are caught by anglers just after ice-out, when the fish move into the shallows to feed in the sun-warmed water. The shallows soon become too warm, sending the fish back to the cold, oxygenated depths. The fish stay deep all summer, until cooler fall weather arrives, when they return to the shallows to feed and spawn.

STATE RECORD: 43 pounds, 8 ounces, Lake Superior (Cook County), 1955

## NORTHERN PIKE
*Esox lucius*

The northern pike (an English name for a pointed, iron-tipped staff, or spear) is a sleek, torpedo-shaped, fish with a long, flat head containing jaws like a duck's bill with rows of needle-sharp, razor-edged teeth that slant back toward the throat.

The northern pike has a legendary appetite, eating up to one-fifth its weight in prey each day and occasionally attacking fish up to one-third its size. When a fish swims past, the northern pike bends back into a C shape, then launches forward openmouthed, slamming the prey and killing it outright or sending it into shock from the trauma. The pike then turns the fish headfirst and swallows it whole in several gluttonous gulps.

The northern pike's teeth have lacerated the fingers of many careless anglers.

STATE RECORD: 45 pounds 12 ounces, Basswood Lake (Lake County), 1929. *This weight, far heavier than any other northern pike caught in Minnesota, is viewed with skepticism by many experienced anglers.*

# The Kawishiwi: A Spirit Land
By Gary Titusdahl

"That's the most amazing thing ever!" we both screamed, almost tipping over our canoe.

"No one will believe this!" my son, Kevin, shouted from the bow as he reached over the side and scooped up the floating Rattlin' Rogue crankbait, holding it high above his head in glee.

"Wait 'til we get home and tell this story." I laughed in disbelief as Kevin tossed the lure to the stern and into my open hands. It's back! Mr. Silver and Orange, my old lucky lure, had miraculously returned from the watery depths. How was this possible?!

Kevin and I were halfway through our eight-day canoe trip into the BWCA. Our campsite was on the Kawishiwi River just north of Malberg Lake in the heart of what we voyageurs call the "pays de'n haut," French for upper country. We were enjoying our 15th summer in a row paddling and fishing these ancient boundary waters. We've explored a lot of territory in those 15 summers. Now, here in the

Kawishiwi wilderness, we were discovering unfamiliar area.

Over the years I had read every book by Sigurd Olson. In "The Singing Wilderness" he wrote about the Kawashaway, known today as Kawishiwi. Olson describes the Kawashaway as a land of mystery. "Bounded by brooding stands of pine, its waters were dark, their origins unknown," he wrote. The Algonquin "Kaw" means "no" and "Ashaway" means "the place between," together meaning "no place between" or spirit land, according to Olson. The Kawashaway belonged to those who had gone before us, he wrote. But it's what he said next that really fueled my fascination – "Strange things have happened there, and the sense of awe and mystery is always present."

When Kevin and I portaged into the Kawishiwi that August morning, two bald eagles flew low over our heads at the landing. A sign from the spirits of the land, we thought. The rolling mist on the river (which I've heard described as "galloping ghosts") felt magical. Then, as we paddled toward our campsite, a humming sound grew louder. A pine tree near the site was totally covered by thousands of bees attracted by pollen, we assumed. It was a "buzzing tree."

After setting up camp, we wondered what awe and mystery might surprise us when we shoved off shore and wet our lines. Time to fish.

Fishing action started out poorly as we worked the edges and patchy weeds, casting topwater baits to try to entice some smallmouth bass. When we drifted near lily pads, I dug deep into my tackle box to bring out my secret weapon Rattlin' Rogue. I always bring it out last. Gives the fish a chance, before I get serious. This favorite lure of mine had never failed me in our six years of partnership. We were best friends.

I let Kevin have the honor of casting it first. Wham! With an explosion, a nice-sized smallie danced its tail on the surface of the water, swinging its head violently, lure on its lips. After a second or two, it dove back into the deep. With Kevin playing the catch carefully, up out of the water came the bass again. At the highest point of its leap, it jerked the bait hard to one side, snapped the line, and plunged back into the lake – with my lure still attached! I was sickened! Not my old trusty! We paddled to the spot, hoping the lure got free and was floating. No such luck. We sat there for several minutes as reality set in. My buddy was gone. Such memories! I half-kiddingly said to Kevin that I wanted to lead a memorial service for our dearly departed, with a prayer and full funeral rights. Maybe sing a hymn like, "Shall We Gather at the River?"

I was mentally writing the eulogy when we heard a loud splash 10 yards behind us. Turning to the sound, we saw that same bass had launched out of the river, flapping in the air, shaking my lure like there was no tomorrow. Then once again it vanished into the depths with lure still in its mouth. With a hoop and a holler we paddled to the spot and peered over the canoe, holding our breath and wanting to believe that lure would surface. Several quiet minutes passed before we gave up hope, smiled, and treasured that one last view of Mr. Silver and Orange. It was an unexpected blessing, we agreed, to have seen it one last time.

Then, the impossible happened! Yet another upheaval just a few yards on the other side of the canoe! That bass was back again, bursting out of the water with more fury this time, twisting at least a foot into the sky, and flipping its head wildly. At its peak, with one last spasm, the fish flung the lure free. My cherished Rattlin' Rogue crankbait plunked down right next to our canoe! What a shock! That's when Kevin leaned over the canoe and swept up old lucky...and we screamed!

Was this a peace offering from the river god who heard our lament? Had the Spirit of Kawishiwi once again moved through this time and place and gifted us with a sense of awe and mystery? Or perhaps the bass was in a defiant spirit. In your face! Take this!

Today my trusty old lure is retired. Missing its lip. Pretty banged up. Still has its rattle, though. I have it mounted on a hall of fame plaque with my other retired all-star fishing lures. It was the best of them all. Whenever I look at it, I think back on that day. Strange things have happened there on the Kawashiwi. I know firsthand its sense of awe and mystery.

## The Finlander

By Barry J. Johnson

My first-ever attempt to catch BWCA lake trout was most likely destined for utter failure. Our four-man crew had never fished for lakers. We had only vague ideas about the gear and tactics needed. To further complicate matters, we were headed to a lake we'd never visited.

Our luck took a turn just after sunrise at a Grand Marais diner, where we wolfed down breakfast and drained mugs of hot coffee to fuel up for the portage in. As the waitress cleared our table, we spread out the map to talk about our destination: Tuscarora Lake. "Tusky" was a "laker lake" according to the research we'd done. We were discussing the portages and speculating about the best campsite on Tusky when a man approached our table.

"Excuse me," the fellow said, "But did I hear you're headed to Tuscarora?" Indeed we were, we confirmed.

"That's my lake. Know it like the back of my hand." He was sturdily built, about our age (30s), wearing a thick wool turtleneck. He introduced himself with one of the most Finnish-sounding names we'd ever heard. I'll just call him "The Finlander."

"You want any tips?" he asked. "Absolutely," we said, "fire away."

He gave us detailed advice and suggestions about the long portages, the preferred campsites, and bait and tackle needed to catch early-spring lake trout. "Have you got salted shiners, water-filled casting bobbers, barrel slip sinkers and good hooks?" We'd never even heard of salted minnows and casting bobbers. We were all ears.

He explained how to salt and preserve minnows for use as lake trout bait. "Nothing hard about it, but it takes a little time to get it right." He continued, "I've got a ton of salted shiners back at my place. They're all packed up and ready to go. I'm happy to set you up with a few dozen, plus the hardware you need. I want to make sure you guys get some lakers, this being your first trip and all."

It seemed too good to be true.

"I've got a seasonal job at one of the resorts up here," he continued. "They give me a room in the bunkhouse, I do building maintenance, carpentry, whatever, and I have plenty of time to fish. Follow me to the resort and I'll set you up."

Our response was half-cautious and half-polite. Maybe, we said, we can just buy what we need at the local bait shop. "We can't ask you to give us a bunch of bait and tackle," we said.

He shook his head, "Bait shops don't have fresh salted shiners. You might find some commercial, pre-packaged ones, but they don't catch much." He furrowed his brow, thinking. Then he played his card. "I tell you what," he announced, "here's another idea. I've got a permit to go into Cross Lake today for some walleye fishing, but I'd MUCH rather catch some lakers. You guys let me tag along with your party and I'll supply the bait and tackle. I'll guide you, and I can almost guarantee you'll catch lakers. I'll clean 'em and cook 'em. I've got all my food and gear packed and ready to go!"

No one expected that, and for a few seconds no one uttered a word. Finally, one of my buddies said, "Sure, come on in with us." That was quickly followed by a second, quieter voice, "Hold on, I don't know about this."

Someone tossed out a good excuse: "We've only got a pair of two-man tents." The Finlander sidestepped that objection, explaining that he rarely used a tent, finding it easier to just crawl into his sleeping bag then roll up in a small tarp.

"I know this is a little weird, but I'm just a fisherman like you," The Finlander assured us. "I'll be no trouble at all, honest. And we'll catch fish. You guys talk it over. If you want to stick with your original plan, I'll still set you up with some shiners."

We needed a crew meeting. We settled our bill, and told the unusual fishing stranger we wanted to head outside to the parking lot and talk as a group.

"No problem," he said, probably believing we were executing a version of the dine-and-dash, never to see him again.

The debate was a classic. We tossed around the pros and the cons and the many unknowns of this unheard-of situation. Who IS this guy? What if he's some kind of freak? This could be really bad. What if he's a decent guy and really knows how to catch lakers? This could be really good.

A few minutes later, we re-entered the restaurant. "You're in," we told The Finlander. "Let's go."

The Finlander was true to his word.

He loaded us up with gear and bait. He outlined his strategy to conquer the killer portages. "We'll take them in increments, maybe a third of a mile at a time," he explained. "I'll tell you when to drop your pack for a rest. We'll switch out who carries the canoe. It seems long, but if we break it down and work as a team it's easy. We'll be there in no time."

The Finlander was a perpetual-motion portage machine, inspiring and cajoling, continuously calling out topography and distances. "Doin' great fellas! You've got a slight rise ahead, but after that, a nice flat stretch! You're about a third of the way done!" He jogged along the trail toting a Duluth pack and a day pack, double-timing from the rear to the front of the portage line. "This guy's a little nuts," I mumbled to my canoe-mate, "but he's good." Eventually, The Finalander dangled the blue carrot: "Just over that next hill, you'll spy the lake through the trees."

He also kept us occupied by telling tales of Tusky. It was 120 feet deep, he said (true). At the top of the lake's food chain were fierce lake trout and predatory northern pike (true). Tusky's deep cold water also held big eelpout (true). He was carrying on the Tusky fishing traditions of his father, Eno, and his grandfather, Urho (who knows?). The lake was named after a rebel breakaway band from the East Coast-based Tuscarora Native American tribe that – for mysterious reasons – split from the larger tribe, migrated west and ended up in the BWCA (complete hogwash).

The Finlander may have carried a pint of whiskey into the woods, or made the journey with a bone-dry pack; my memory on that point is dim. If he did carry a bottle, it wasn't enough. What I vividly recall is his thirst. It was oceanic, unquenchable.

"Hey, can you spare a bump?" he'd ask at the first sight of a Nalgene filled with booze. Once our friendship started to coalesce, he'd holler "Give a man a drink!" or "What in the HELL does a guy have to do to get served in this joint!?" When you did mix him a drink, he'd drain half the cup, hand it back to you with a big smile and ask, "Top me off?"

The Finlander helped empty every bottle in sight, but the whiskey was a bargain for the fishing gear and guidance he delivered. He patiently taught us how to tie laker rigs and hook the salted minnows, which he supplied in abundance. He positioned us along the shoreline and advised where to cast. When – as he'd promised – we began to hook, fight and land lakers, he seemed happier than we were. We kept a few to eat, but released most of them.

One cold, gray, windy afternoon, The Finlander asked "How 'bout some fish chowder to warm us up?" Digging into his pack, he pulled out a few potatoes and an onion, which he chopped and began to fry. Next, he deftly skinned a freshly caught lake trout, then sliced the fillets into deep-orange finger-thin pieces. To the fish and vegetables, he added a pair of powdered soup mixes – cream of potato and broccoli, as I recall – plus salt and pepper and maybe a dash of cayenne pepper. He topped it off with a few quarts of water and put it on the boil. We tossed some logs on the fire, and sat around talking as the chowder bubbled and thickened. The chill in the air amplified the steam rolling off the pot.

In time, The Finlander ladled up bowls of fresh Lake Trout Chowder. It had few ingredients, but in that odd way of the wilderness, sometimes the simplest foods land on the tongue as impossibly rare delicacies, so precious they can't be had at any cost, at any restaurant.

And in this case, I suppose, that was true. The steaming, delicious soup was the culmination of a true "what-are-the-odds" meeting of a BWCA character we'll never forget. *Here's to the Finlander!* (Don't forget to top off his drink after the toast.)

## *Perfect Timing on Vern River*
By Kent Kaiser

One spring, John, a friend from out East who was about to finish grad school at the University of Minnesota, asked if I would arrange a Boundary Waters canoe trip before he moved away to take a professorship. He was an experienced outdoorsman but had never been to the BWCA.

John wanted to catch fish, which I thought should not be difficult. Joining us would be three other graduate students (all BWCA greenhorns), and a friend of John's, who was an experienced camper. It was a two-night trip. Consequently, I knew the route would have to be easy and short. I thought about a route I had not traveled in several years: enter at Homer Lake, north of Tofte, then head into Vern Lake.

The three grad students were utterly unprepared and ill-suited for a canoe trip. Their gear was not well packed. They brought practically no food, but made sure to haul in a huge bottle of hard liquor. Their tent was huge – it had an attached screen porch. They wanted that big tent to themselves, which turned out to be a good decision.

After starting on Homer Lake and making two ridiculously short portages, we were on Vern Lake. We could see that the nearest campsite was open, and we grabbed it. In the hundred-or-so-yard paddle to the campsite, one of our inexperienced campers dropped his fishing rod overboard into the deep dark water, which would have ended his fishing before it started, except that John had brought extra gear.

After setting up camp, we decided to try fishing on Vern Lake and had a little luck with small northern and decent-sized smallmouth bass, even right from the campsite. Indeed, we caught enough so that the provision-less members of our party did not have to go hungry that evening.

The next day, we decided to fish the length of Vern Lake, and we caught only a few little bass. We returned to camp, and everyone wanted a nap. I was refreshed after dozing for a few minutes, and I wanted to try some evening fishing. I couldn't roust anyone else, so I went solo. I paddled the Vern River, where I had caught some fish in the past. It was a beautiful, calm, sunny evening — one of those perfect days we all dream about in canoe country. Like many rivers in the boundary waters, the Vern River at this point consists of lake-like stretches of relatively deep, fishable water, with rapids every so often.

I trolled with a Rapala and picked up a couple of northern pike too small to keep. Downstream, there are many tiny islands, rock outcroppings, weedbeds and sunken logs. I didn't catch anything as I made my first pass down the river. I turned around to start my paddle back to camp, since it was getting late. Just then, I hooked a fish. Much to my surprise, it turned out to be a beautiful, three-pound walleye. I didn't think such a nice fish existed in this little river.

Back at camp, everyone else was now awake. John had caught a couple of smallies from the campsite. Unfortunately, he had also embedded a hook (including the barb) into the skin between the thumb and index finger on his right hand. He'd pushed the hook through the skin to expose the barb. Looking at it made the one medical school student too queasy to help, so John had waited for me to return. Thankfully, we had a Leatherman tool in camp, and I clipped the barb, allowing John to extract the hook, though not without significant bleeding.

That evening, we had a great fish dinner, and John and I turned in relatively early. We would fish the Vern River at sun-up. Meanwhile, our inexperienced trip partners stayed up late around the campfire and drank heavily. We knew they would be in no condition to get up early in the morning. It occurred to me that they were actually on a completely different canoe trip than I was.

John and I did, in fact, wake up early. There was bit of fog over the lake, but we could tell it was going to be another bright, sunny day. We headed down the river to try for walleyes. We worked the area for a while, with no luck.

John thought we should try casting for smallmouth around some of the numerous rock outcroppings and small islands, so we headed for one. John cast his lure right next to an island, and – bam! – a nice smallie grabbed it. He landed a four-pounder. After a few unsuccessful casts, we headed to another little island. Same thing: First cast and bam! Another nice smallie. Again, it seemed to be the only fish next to this rock outcropping. We moved to the next little island, and, again, a nice fish. We repeated this tactic again, and again, and again. Sometimes I caught a fish, but for the most part, I paddled the canoe into position so John could make the cast. Several times it seemed as if John cast his lure directly onto the fish, they hit so quickly.

The way John put it, after the earlier mediocre fishing: "This is what I expected Boundary Waters fishing to be like." As is often the case with BWCA fishing, the timing was everything. We were fortunate to have found the fish when we did, for this was the last day of our trip, and we soon commenced packing our gear to leave.

## One Less Duck
By Roxanne Chmielewski

My BWCA trips leave me with a wonderful memory of beauty, peace, the wonder of nature, the appreciation of hard physical work, and the joy of friendship. Also, an enduring love of the flora and fauna of the North Woods. I've viewed creatures that are difficult to see when motors and noise are involved.

One stark memory is sitting on a rock on an island in Lake Saganaga at dusk. I casually watch as a duck and her half-grown ducklings swim just offshore. Next, I see a huge dark shadow coming up under the ducks, and a duckling simply disappears with a swoosh. A good meal for a monster fish, but one less duck. I recall that the attack was so swift and nearly silent that the other ducks did not seem to notice or be fearful.

## An Unexpected Gift
By Mark Peters

The year was '66, I was college freshman looking for a summer job, and my buddy Rod, Minnesota's first hippie (though he had no idea he was), could get one for me through his father … but there was a catch. Rod needed a partner for a fishing and canoe trip in the Arrowhead Region as celebration for finishing high school. If I wanted the job, I had to do the trip.

We fished from Tom Lake to the Fowls on the Canadian border and threw in a couple of streams for good measure. All we had to show for our time was three pike, two brook trout and a largemouth bass. By our last day you'd have thought Rod had lice for the head scratching he did.

It was then he pulled out his trump card, a lake he'd never fished and nobody at the post office or the gas stations would talk about: East Pike Lake. Back in '66 East Pike wasn't as yet in the BWCA. That didn't happen until '77.

Seeing East Pike for the first time, we stopped and strung up our rods. I tied on a Bass-o-Reno lure and gave it a fling.

Bam! Two-pound smallmouth. Think we were excited? An unknown lake at our feet, no doubt filled with eager bass. We spent two hours hammering smallies on the downwind side of the lake. In the rising breeze, Rod and I took turns with fishing, camera work, and boat control. The morning sparkled, the waves glistened, and the overly fertile females, just now moving onto their beds wouldn't ignore anything thrown in their direction.

We found the ladies in the shade, tucked in tight to shore. They shunned small plugs and ignored a slow, twitchy retrieve. They'd explode off their beds before the poor, unsuspecting lure had a chance to hit the water and make its moves. For couple of exciting hours we threw them the biggest plugs we had, cranked 'em in as soon as they hit the water, then held on for all we were worth. The smallies average size neared three pounds with Rod hooking the largest at close to five. Come noon the action stopped cold. Near exhausted, I put my rod down, leaned back, and lit up.

The next morning we packed our gear in the Chevy and headed home. A half-century later, I can close my eyes and conjure up the vision of that first cast exactly as it was, smell the overhanging sunlit cedars, see the deadfall pines joining the shallows to the shore, and hear the splash of the waves as they slid over the baseball-sized rocks lining the bottom. I went back, but not for 26 years. My 12-year-old son Allan stood beside me. And the memory of that second moment is as clear as the first.

# BWCA QUIZ #2

**1.)** What was not widely found in the BWCA prior to about 1920?

**2.)** The highest point in Minnesota is in the BWCA. What is it, and how tall is it?

**3.)** The town of Ely didn't always have that name. What was it originally called?

**4.)** Who or what is the Sawbill Trail named after?

**5.)** What is the literal French meaning of the term "Voyaguer"?

### BWCA Quiz #2 – Answers

1.) Largemouth and smallmouth bass are not native to BWCA lakes. They were deliberately stocked during the 1920s, '30s and '40s.

2.) Eagle Mountain, about 21.5 miles north of Lutsen, MN, sits just inside the BWCA. Eagle Mountain rises to 2,301 feet above sea level.

3.) Ely started out as "Florence," Minnesota. It was soon discovered that another Minnesota town was already named Florence. The name was then changed to Ely. Ely who? Some people say Samuel B. Ely, a Michigan miner who championed the potential of the Vermillion Iron Range; others say Arthur Ely, a railroad man who helped create the Duluth & Iron Range Railroad.

4.) The trail is named after the Common Merganser Duck, which goes by the nickname "Sawbill."

5.) The term translates as "traveler."

# MISADVENTURES & MISHAPS

## *Buggy Encounters in the BWCA*
By guest author Dr. Bruce Giebink

*Dr. Bruce Giebink (aka Bruce the Bug Guy) owns and operates "The Bug Zone, LLC." Dr. Giebink earned his doctorate in Entomology from the University of Wisconsin-Madison. He later served as an Assistant Professor at the University of Minnesota. Dr. Giebink has published various scientific and popular publications on insects, has advised teachers on insect curricula and is an energetic public speaker on many insect-related topics. He can be reached at: 6676 Sandhill Drive, Lino Lakes MN 55014; 651-780-8216; bugzone@comcast.net; or www.brucethebugguy.net.*

You're finally here, in this special wilderness area called the Boundary Waters Canoe Area. It's a gorgeous spring day and you're excited about exploring this amazing area by canoe.

Then WHAM, something jabs you in the back of the neck! You reflexively grab your neck and feel some hard little bumps. You spot blood on your fingers. You reach back again to pick at one of the "bumps" and discover that the "bump" is actually a tiny hard-bodied fly, called a black fly (and a number of other less complimentary names!). You glance down and notice your jeans are covered with other tiny flies. In fact, they seem to be EVERYWHERE! What the heck! How did they find you so fast! The fact is, you unwittingly "attracted" them by wearing blue jeans (blue is a favorite color of these vicious little dipterans, a.k.a. flies).

But they're not content to simply rest on your jeans. Oh no! They're female black flies and to them you're a warm-blooded creature who can provide exactly what they need to raise a family: BLOOD! Try to not take it too personally. Any moose, deer, mouse or bird would actually be better, because they have "higher quality" blood (human blood is low in isoleucine, an amino acid needed to build egg proteins). But, if a human is available, these bugs can't resist biting. They're just doing their job; it's what they NEED to do!

As you probably know, the dreaded black fly is not the only blood-thirsty bug in the North Woods. A number of other biting flies annoy canoeists to no end. The flies (Order Diptera = two wings) are probably the most annoying and troublesome insects on the planet.

Here in the North Woods, our most notorious winged tormentors are the aquatic Diptera, such as mosquitoes, black flies, biting gnats or no-see-ums, and certain Tabanids, such as deer flies and horse flies. They are called aquatic diptera because in their larval or immature stages, they live and develop in water. In a water-rich environment such as the BWCA, you'll need to be prepared to put up with (and – as much as possible – protect yourself from) these cursed flies, which at times can reach plague-like proportions.

In reality, there are thousands of species of insects in the North Woods. Why is it that these particular types of flies cause us so much grief? Remember, every mosquito, black fly, biting gnat, no-see-um, deer fly and horse fly that bites you is a female. While these ladies are only doing what comes naturally to them, they are the most annoying and disliked of all the insects. The female flies require a blood meal to properly develop their eggs. Males do NOT bite, but instead feed on plant nectars for nourishment. Females also depend on high-energy plant nectars for their active lifestyle, but must obtain the protein from blood for egg development.

### MOSQUITOES

The term mosquito comes from the Latin word *Mosca*, which later became *mosquito* or *mosquita*, which means "little fly" in Spanish and Portuguese. There are 52 different species of mosquitos in Minnesota, the worst biters being *Aedes vexans* and the cattail mosquito. You can tell a male from a female by looking at the antennae. Females have thread-like antennae; males have bushy, fuzzy antennae. Note: Crane flies look a LOT like mosquitoes and many folks mistakenly think of these long-legged flies as "giant mosquitoes." But they don't bite. In fact, they typically live only a few days and seldom eat.

How do mosquitoes find us? And what can we do to make ourselves harder to find or less appealing to mosquitoes? Like many insects, mosquitoes live primarily in a chemical world and find us (or any other warm-blooded victim) by encountering chemical and physical cues that we give off: carbon dioxide, lactic acid, natural skin oils and heat. We all give off these cues, but alas, some unfortunate folks give off stronger cues than others. They've been called "mosquito- or bug-magnets."

One of the best ways to fool biting insects is by masking our odors, which is how insect repellents work. The most effective repellents are those containing the chemical DEET. Most of us are familiar with various commercial products which contain different percentages of DEET.

Some of the other ways people have tried to to repel Skeeters include: skin lotions, citronella candles, citrosa plants, spicy foods and B1 vitamins, geraniums, chrysanthemums, propane foggers, mosquito coils, sonic devices, bug zappers, etc. From a scientific perspective, all of these preventatives are questionable.

Here are my recommendations to help you reduce your appeal as bug bait (NOTE: many of these tactics also apply to black flies, no-see-ums, horse flies and deerflies):

- Wear loose clothing (this provides a pocket of protection around you).
- Wear white or drab-colored clothing; the shinier the better!
- Cover your head by wearing a light-colored hat.
- Never wear red or blue; this is like inviting bugs to dinner!
- Tuck your pants into your socks (also recommended in tick season). Even if you look like a dork, you'll be a more comfortable, less tormented dork!
- Stay in your tent at dusk and dawn, which are peak feeding times for mosquitoes.
- Refrain from wearing a lot of fragrant lotions, perfume or scented hairsprays.
- To repel "clouds" of bugs, add a little wet wood or pine boughs to the campfire; the smoke will keep nearby mosquitoes at bay.

## BLACK FLIES

How can such a tiny fly be so evil?! Black flies are commonly called biting gnats (and worse!) and are closely related to mosquitoes. They are also called buffalo gnats because their stout, humpbacked profile and two hornlike antennae give them the appearance of miniature (flying) buffalos.

Like mosquitoes, female black flies suck blood in order to develop their eggs. But they do this with much less finesse than mosquitoes. Whereas Skeeters have syringe-like mouthparts designed to pierce capillaries, black flies tear a hole in the skin with their saw-toothed mandibles and then suck up blood from the oozing pool.

BWCA black flies are most abundant during spring and early summer, sometimes in plague-like swarms. A few remain present throughout the summer. They're active during the day, with peak biting periods during the morning and early evening. Bites are painful and itchy, characterized by a reddened weal with a wound in the center. Thankfully, black flies in Minnesota do NOT transmit any diseases to humans.

In addition to the bug-avoidance tactics listed earlier, use these tips to discourage black flies:

- Apply insect repellent to your neck, behind your ears, under your chin, around your wrists and around your ankles.
- If bitten, avoid scratching. Use anti-itch products to alleviate some of the discomfort.

## NO-SEE-UMS

You may not see these nasty little creatures very well, but they sure have a way of getting your attention! Some are so small they can pass through window screens! To entomologists, these tiny flies are the Ceratopogonids — variously known as biting midges, no-see-ums, punkies, gnats or moose flies.

Until they mercilessly start hacking and slashing at your skin, you might ignore them as little (harmless) tiny flies. Once they have your attention (if you take the time before slapping them) you'll notice that they have a Quasimodo-like hump on their back (between their head and wings) that projects over the head.

Again, the female is after your blood. But they get it more violently than a mosquito. Whereas the mosquito is more like an acupuncturist, who accurately and painlessly pierces the skin, the no-see-um is like a scissor-hands-monster run amuck, cutting and slashing the skin with its scissor-like mandibles and then sucking up the resulting pool of blood. Painful and messy!

**DEER FLIES AND HORSE FLIES**

There's nothing sneaky or subtle about these huge-eyed flies! They are big, noisy and extremely persistent. Some people consider deer flies and horseflies THE most annoying insects in the North Woods! They will hover endlessly around your head, buzzing irritatingly and waiting for an opportunity get a blood meal from you. The female flies want to jab you with their dagger-like mouthparts, sip some of your blood and be on their way.

If you're in a canoe, you're essentially horsefly bait, especially if your ankles are exposed. Horseflies are bigger than deer flies, so they are slower and easier to whack when they land on you.

Enjoy your visit to this wonderful place, but prepare yourself: pack plenty of insect repellent, long khaki pants, long-sleeved shirts and a hat to minimize your exposure to and discomfort from these "bad elements" of the North Woods.

## *How to Wreck a Canoe*
By Donald Marpe

Once in a while, common sense seems to evaporate and something gets broken, such as a canoe getting bent out of shape. That's not best thing to happen when you're nine miles and half a dozen portages away from your car.

One of my favorite places for a short trip is Lake Agnes by way of the Nina-Moose River, especially if all you have is three or four days and you'd like to fish more than travel. The fishing is usually pretty good and, if you set up camp on Lake Agnes, there are several other options for day trips, such as the Oyster Lake chain or on up to Lac La Croix. So that's the trip six of us, all engineers who worked at a computer company, planned for a Labor Day weekend. (To protect the innocent, most of the names which follow are not the names given them by their mothers.)

Of this group, I'd been to the Boundary Waters once with Vince and I knew nothing of the experience level of any of the other four. Our plans were to take three canoes. Vince and I would partner in mine, Dick and Jim would have Dick's fairly new 17-foot Grumman, and we'd pick up a canoe in Ely for Rob and Tommy.

After a day of fishing on Lake Agnes we decided to go up to Lac la Croix for our last full day. The portage at the Nina-Moose River and Lake Agnes isn't very long, but to Dick and Jim, the rapids looked much more attractive; the urge to run them was too much to resist.

We had walked the portage and seen the large pine tree laying across the river about mid-portage. When we drew Dick's attention to this, he said they'd stop there and portage around it. They did reluctantly follow the advice given to unload their fishing tackle and other gear from the canoe and they agreed to wait until the rest of us could get positioned where we could observe their "feat" just upstream from the big pine tree.

Down the river came Dick and Jim with paddles poised to keep them off any rocks that might appear. I'm sure both were surprised at how fast the current flowed. They'd badly miscalculated their plan to exit the river before they got to the pine tree. The canoe slammed head on into the trunk of the tree, right in the center of the river, and before they could react, the canoe swung around so it lay against the tree trunk perpendicular to the current. For a moment or two they might have had a chance to save it but they both thought they should get out of the canoe. In doing so, the canoe tipped into the current and immediately filled with water. That was the end of that canoe – it folded in the middle (forming a horrible "V" shape) and became wedged under the pine tree. Dick and Jim were standing waist deep in the river.

Since the canoe couldn't be budged, Dick started calling for someone to "throw me an axe," forgetting that we were on a day trip and the axe was back in camp at the far end of Lake Agnes. When he saw we weren't making any effort to help him but, in fact, were having difficulty keeping ourselves from laughing, he got mad. Perhaps it was wrong of us to laugh but until the canoe folded up this was the most hilarious comedy any of us had seen in a long while. Eventually the canoe was freed up and we helped drag it up on the bank where we were partially successful in unfolding the canoe so the angle of the forward half to the aft half was only about 30 degrees, rather than 90. The front half was also twisted out of alignment so this was really a "compound" bend and certainly fatal for the canoe.

We'd stopped laughing when we realized the canoe was wrecked but we could tell that Dick was still pretty mad at us. We leaned the canoe against a large tree and built a fire so Dick and Jim could warm up. We continued to try to straighten the canoe but someone started laughing again which only made Dick madder. Now it really became funny, at least we thought so. Another party crossing the portage joined in on the laughing. Dick was not happy.

Dick could see he wasn't going to get sympathy from any of us so he put his wet clothes back on and jammed his hat on his head. He did a pretty good lift of his canoe onto his shoulders, considering the new orientation of the canoe yoke, and grabbed his paddle. When he got back to the lake he dropped the canoe in, tossed his paddle into the canoe and jumped in himself. We thought the canoe probably leaked badly but as Dick paddled away we could see that the front half of the canoe was not in the water while the rear half just rode a little lower with Dick's weight. He seemed to be heading back to our camp but he wouldn't speak to us so we thought it best to just let him go. We stood around the fire until Jim got a little drier and then we decided it was too late to go on to Lac La Croix and anyway, maybe we should follow up on Dick to make sure he made it back to camp.

When we got back to camp Dick's canoe was pulled up on the rocks; he'd made it back OK. Apparently the back half of the canoe hadn't leaked too much. It appeared Dick was in his tent but he refused to answer anyone when we tried to talk to him. In fact, he stayed silently in his tent all that evening. The next morning he rolled out of the tent and, without a word, shoved off for the river in his bent-up canoe. He'd left all his gear in the tent, so everything he brought, including the tent, came back with us.

As we paddled out, we met another party just heading in. They'd seen Dick and his odd watercraft, and when they asked him what happened to his canoe they received a very discourteous answer. We caught up with Dick on the next-to-last portage but he still wouldn't talk to us. At the take-out site, we still got the silent treatment and when we stopped in Ely for a good meal

Dick stayed in Jim's car and wouldn't join us.

Our relationship at work with Dick didn't change much over the next few weeks but after his insurance agent called about his brand new canoe, he managed to tell us all about it. Maybe we shouldn't have laughed at his misfortune, but even today, 40 years later, I can't recall that adventure without chuckling.


## *A Pre-Marriage Lesson*

By Lisa & Duncan (last name withheld by request of the authors)

It was an unusually chilly spring weekend when my fiancé, Duncan, and I drove north for our first BWCA experience together in May 2009. We were to be married in a few short months, so we thought a long weekend in the beautiful outdoors would allow us to relax and ignore the wedding planning for a few days. Boy, were we in for a surprise!

After a few hours of paddling, we found a perfect, private campsite. Prior to the trip, I explicitly asked that we find a secluded site, and this one delivered! Duncan lodged the Kevlar canoe between two large trees near the shore. I cautioned him against it (my preference would have been to pull the canoe up right next to the tent), but he reminded me that I tend to worry about worst-case scenarios (I am my father's daughter), and he said the canoe would be fine. It was a lovely, calm evening, so no need to worry.

Famous last words.

A storm blew in and strong winds rocked and rattled our tiny tent. I was so concerned about trees falling on us I didn't even think about the canoe.

The CANOE! Our lifeline! Our link back to civilization!

The next morning I beelined to the shore and the canoe was gone. Hoping for the best, I asked Duncan, "Honey, did you move the canoe?" He furrowed his brows, then looked down to the shore. Our canoe had disappeared.

Our eyes searched the perimeter of the lake, hoping to see that big yellow belly of a canoe bulging out on the shoreline. Nothing.

I sat down on the nearest log and bit my lip to avoid the words, "I TOLD YOU SO!" from escaping. We each took a moment to experience the emotions that come with the realization of being stranded in the wilderness, then decided to work together to make a plan.

1. We had enough food for a four-day weekend. We needed to start rationing.
2. Our campsite was secluded so we risked not seeing other campers who could help us unless we moved to a more visible location.

My gut told me to get comfortable and stay put. The Forest Service would come find us in a few days. However, my future husband is a go-getter who likes to take control of a situation, so staying put and waiting for someone to find us wasn't an option.

We bundled up, packed supplies and grabbed our canoe paddles to help bush-whack through the woods (luckily we had hauled the paddles up next to the tent).The woods were SO thick and we got battered and bruised trying to navigate around up-rooted trees, through thicket and fallen branches, as we slowly battled our way to a better destination in hopes of flagging down paddlers.

At a peninsula, we weathered rain, high winds, snow and sleet as we waited, waited, waited. We saw no one. Not a single canoe. We hollered, whistled and yelled for help, but the winds were too strong and loud and there was no one to hear us anyway.

The next day we muscled our way back to the peninsula, again hoping to find help. To avoid getting further battered and bruised, we attempted a different route and found ourselves seriously LOST. Feelings of real, visceral fear and desperation set in.

We back-tracked along the shore and ultimately found our way to the peninsula. After I shed a few pitiful tears, Duncan and I agreed it was best to stay at the campsite, where we had shelter and comfort. We were supposed to be back at work that day, so we believed a rescue effort should be set in motion soon.

At the campsite, we decided to make the most of the situation and try to have some fun. The weather had improved and the sun broke through the clouds. Duncan had fishing line and carved a bobber out of some driftwood (most of his fishing gear had been strapped to the missing canoe). He captured a crayfish to use as bait and caught a beautiful smallmouth bass. We felt like true survivors at that moment.

As he cooked the fish over the campfire, something caught

his eye – a flash in the distance. He jumped up and started yelling and waving his arms like a lunatic, and when I realized there was a canoe headed our way, tears started streaming down my cheeks. We jumped and hugged and hollered together. We were going to be saved!

Two older gentlemen – the Haney brothers from Wisconsin – told us they had seen our canoe. Someone brought it to a portage and left a note: "Watch for stranded campers." We got our canoe back!!

It was late afternoon when we were rescued, so we decided to stay one more night. We fished, we jumped in the frigid lake, we saw moose swim past our campsite, we FEASTED (appetizer: Rye crackers with sausage and Babybel cheese; entrée: two bags of Raman noodles covered with freeze-dried Kung-Pao Chicken; dessert: hot chocolate with a shot of Scotch to warm our bellies).

We also made sure to tie up the canoe very securely that night.

When we reminisce about the experience of being stranded in the BWCA for six days, Duncan always shares the lesson he learned: "My wife is always right. If she says, 'Tie up the canoe,' you tie up the canoe. If she says, 'I think we should stay at the campsite to get rescued,' you stay at the campsite." And that is marriage advice that continues to serve us well!

## A Camp Counselor's Guide to Surviving the BWCA (Without Dying in Rapids in the Process)
By Beth Harrell

"Oh Dear God!" These were the last words I heard from my fellow canoe partner as the roar of the rapids overcame us. The branch I had been holding onto had slipped through my fingers, propelling us forward toward a 30-foot length of churning whitewater coursing over and past huge boulders.

As our canoe floated backwards down the rapids, I watched the horrified faces of the rest of our party, safe on dry land. While I could see them shouting at us, all I could hear was the sound of rushing water, as well as the sound of my boss' voice in my mind, calling my parents to tell them I was dead. At that moment I would have rather been in any other BWCA predicament: swarmed by mosquitoes; portaging for 20 miles; or even being attacked by a gang of rogue beavers.

While the idea of exploring rapids had seemed exciting five minutes ago, we learned quickly that we had made a foolish and impulsive mistake. As camp counselors from a Northern Minnesota camp, we had embarked together on a two-day Boundary Waters trip as part of our staff orientation.

On the second and final day of our trip, we came across a friendly stranger who warned us of unmarked rapids that lay ahead. We thanked him for the information and promptly disregarded the warning. Continuing on in the direction of the rapids, we were eager to take the fastest shortcut in order to make up for distance lost waiting out some rain that morning. We were excited for an adventure and the rapids did not look dangerous at first glance.

As we continued, we realized we had made a terrible mistake: a 30-foot section of nasty water loomed ahead of us, and panic struck. The current – gentle up to this point – was quickly gathering momentum and the sound of cascading water was drawing near. The drop was narrow and deep, sharply curving to the left, with many jagged rocks and branches jutting out. We risked not only capsizing and damaging or losing our equipment, but serious injury and possible death.

Two of the three canoes in our party safely veered off to dry ground. The canoe I was steering was drawn mercilessly downstream toward the drop. My mind raced with worst-case scenarios: I pictured our canoe speeding into the rapids, my head striking a rock and later a moose discovering my dead body.

Finally, through effort and luck, we were able to reach the opposite bank before the plummet. There, I clung onto a tree branch for dear life. We listened as our teammates shouted instructions, yet in an instant the branch slipped through my fingers. The canoe began to float backward down the rapids. In desperation, one of my passengers flung herself onto a rock just feet away from the thundering fall of cascading water. Our canoe became wedged between two rocks, and we were able to find an area shallow enough to disembark and drag our canoe to shore. As soon as we made it safely back on land we knew a celebration was in order (also, I personally had to change my shorts).

It's often said that shortcuts cost more time in the end. Since that day I have refused to take shortcuts, whether physically or metaphorically speaking. The lessons I learned in the Boundary Waters impacted not only my summer, but my life as well. One key lesson: Relationships are best cultivated basking in the sun, but they are best strengthened in the rapids.

## A Thin Blue Line on the Map
By Chuck Rose

Trail Creek! This was the day. For years (off and on, but literally years) we had looked suspiciously at the thin blue line on the map linking Trail Lake with the Maligne River. Had people been there before? Undoubtedly. How many? Inquiries suggested very few. Would the creek be passable? Today, we would find out.

It was Roger and Larry's idea. Get some friends together – Boy Scout guides who had worked at the Charles L. Sommer Wilderness Canoe Base – and go to extra-adventurous places in the Quetico. They had recruited Don and me, as well as Roger's dog, Thor (another Quetico veteran). The trip so far had taken us from Moose Lake, in the middle of the Boundary Waters, northwest to Quetico Lake where we turned south to start our serpentine route back. We were camped on Your Lake. Breaking camp early, we loaded our Seliga canoes and headed for the eastern end of the lake.

Joe Seliga made wood/canvas canoes in Ely from 1938 to 2005. In 1993, when Roger went to pick up his new Seliga canoe, Larry had put his name on the waiting list. Three years later, Larry had his prize as well. Now both their forest-green, mahogany-trimmed canoes glided along on the smooth lake under overcast skies. Our trip began on the first of June in the hope that there would be enough water along the thin blue line. Of course, we were always careful not to damage our canoes, because they were our precious lifelines, because of their beauty, and because we didn't want to be driving back through Ely and have Joe see scratches on one his creations.

We portaged to Snow, then Little Pine Lake. Thor supervised. To borrow (and localize) an old mariners' quote: "Beavers be here." Trail Creek widened as we approached our first dam, over which we were able to lift the canoes. Thor supervised. Another bend and the creek became a trickle through a wide gravel bed. Time to portage, then paddle to the next beaver dam. We had to unload our packs from the canoe before lifting over the dam. No scratches that time. Careful. Repeat.

OWWW! A branch on a beaver log poked through the side of Roger's canoe. Fabric ripped. At least it was above the water line. Thor supervised. Between six and what seemed like 20,000,000 dams later, we felt we must be near the end. We gazed over the next dam to find ... mud. A dam downstream must have gone out. We were on our own. The left bank had more open meadow, so onto our shoulders went the packs and canoes for the final stretch to the Maligne River. Four hours of toil, a bit over four miles (not counting zig-zags), and we had survived Trail Creek. Without our buddies the beavers, there would have never been enough water to make it. Time for lunch. Roger duct-taped the six-inch tear in his canvas. Thor supervised.

On the Maligne, just upstream from us, was Tanner Lake, named for John Tanner, stolen as a young boy in Kentucky to take the place of a Shawnee mother's dead son. He became famous by his Indian name *White Falcon*. John was shot and left for dead on "his" lake, because of a dispute on whether his daughters should attend a white school. He was rescued by passing Voyageurs.

Loading the canoes, we moved downstream on the Maligne; it was difficult to tell where Trail Creek came out. Meeting the Darky River we turned south – upstream – then did multiple small portages up the river to Minn Lake. Camping on an island, nobody had the energy to go out fishing that night; instead, we played cribbage. Roger and Thor turned in early.

The rest of the trip was a pleasure as we traveled through McAree, Argo, Ted, McIntyre, Cecil, Kett, and Basswood before ending at Fall Lake, near Ely.

So what makes me look back on this day so fondly? New territory, a challenge completed, the wildlife, good company, the Seligas. We would have traveled over those beaver dams faster if we had aluminum or even kelvar canoes. But while protecting the canvas, we were more aware of our surroundings, paying attention to every rock and stick. Imagine what it would be like to paddle (and portage) a birch bark canoe through such a maze.

Would I go back again? I'd prefer to try Wildgoose Creek (new territory and there rumors of brook trout).


## BWCA 101
By Mac Meade

I originally tried a solo BWCA canoe trip for many reasons; maybe most importantly it allowed me to make rookie mistakes without anyone else seeing.

My brother-in-law loaned me his 17-foot Alumacraft for my maiden solo. The canoe had enough room for three people and their packs, and probably weighed 75 pounds.

My camping experience was grounded in backpacking, so my gear was an external frame pack, fishing rod, and a paddle. I loaded my light gear into the canoe immediately in front of my seat in the stern, and pushed off into the choppy water of Snowbank Lake.

I wasn't on the water long before I noticed the water ripple up and move toward my bow from ahead left.

**Lesson #1:** When the surface of the water ripples and the ripples appear to be moving toward you, the wind is about to kick your butt. The ripples hit the bow of my canoe and before I could react, the accompanying gust swung my bow 180-degrees. I was now facing the shore.

I tried to turn the canoe around, digging in one side then quickly back-paddling on the other. Regardless what I did or how hard I paddled, I could not turn my bow against the wind. I nearly wore myself out trying to beat that damn wind before realizing it was futile. I relinquished, paddling back to the shore, where I turned the canoe around, and once again pushed off.

Sure enough, a couple of hundred feet from shore, another ripple gusted toward me. But this time I was ready. When it hit my bow, I was already paddling like a mad man, bound to keep 'er heading the right direction. This time I won the battle.The gust moved on and I was able to continue, now probably 300 yards into the lake, a bit off line but back on course.

The further I moved out into the lake, the heavier the gusts. But I was dog-determined not to lose my bow to the wind. I am sure more than a few people on the lake heard the top-of-my-lungs expletives flowing during my episodes of frantic paddling.

As I moved from ripples to whitecaps, I quickly learned **Lesson #2:** Keep your nose pointed into the wind.

With my bow into the wind, I watched for gusts on the water ahead. I'd ease up between the gusts, and then kick up my mad paddling as each blast tried to turn me. In this way I tacked the wind, allowing it to push my bow just off center of the wind direction, as I paddled against that push. If I worked it correctly, I could paddle hard on the same side of the canoe for long periods of time.

This generally worked, but there were times when the wind was so strong it would push me broadside, me pulling water as if my life depended on it. I would battle that way until my arms ached to prevent the canoe from turning past 90 degrees. If I let the nose slip past 90 degrees to the wind, I would quickly be turned 180 degrees, staring back from whence I came. That too happened, and the effort required to get my bow back into the wind in the middle of the lake was ridiculous.

It was two, maybe three hours of my man-vs.-nature battle before I finally made it to the portage, completely drained. I must have been a sight as I worked my way back and forth across the lake, but I survived, proud of myself for doing so.

A canoeist standing on the portage struck up a conversation as I pulled up. "I saw you battling the wind out there," he said to me.

"It was brutal," I replied. "I'm exhausted."

"Yes, I can imagine," he said. "You might want to consider putting some weight in your bow."

**Lesson #3.**


## *The Great Paddle Theft of 2005*
By Kate Hathaway

In my cousins' house there is an entire wall dedicated to the memory of Boundary Waters' trips. It is covered with collages, each full of photographs from a specific trip. The wall now includes 18 collages, with one more added each year.

Most often the trips include a guest, and in 2005 I was the guest. During a "layover" on "Wind Chill" (a.k.a. Winchell Lake) my cousin and I took off across the lake to look for better firewood. We pulled the canoe ashore before heading back into the woods. We were gone quite a while exploring, and although we heard scuffling on the shoreline behind us, we did not think to look back (because, of course, you are taught to look FORWARD when in the BWCA!).

Upon return to our craft, we quickly noted that something was amiss – no paddles! We immediately spotted two cousins canoing swiftly back across the lake toward our campsite, with our paddles resting inside their canoe. This left us, the hardworking wood-finders, stranded.

Perhaps our previous three days of wilderness challenges helped our creative processes. Within minutes, we decided against granting the thieves any satisfaction for their blade pilfering. The Superior National Forest provided us ample timber. Back to the woods we went, with a towrope and saw. Forty-five minutes later we had constructed paddles that were rustic but functional. They were also unbelievably heavy! Our upper bodies were well-exercised by the time we arrived back in camp – with dry firewood *and* a grand sense of satisfaction.

We enjoyed the confused looks of the thieves, and the entire group's befuddlement at how we had managed to paddle back across the lake, which became clear only as we chugged closer to the campsite. The laughter went all around, with praise for the problem-solving skills of the avenged victims, and compliments for the creative thieves.

Featured in our photo collage from that year are shots of two logs, crudely hewn into a form that provided a pair of determined young explorers transportation across a lake.

Although we are firm believers in leaving in the BWCA that which belongs there, somehow these log paddles made it home in the back of the van, and for several years graced my cousin's bedroom with their beauty – a reminder of the joy of family camaraderie and the lessons that can be learned only with time to learn them and a wilderness and loving company ready to supply us with the opportunities.

# A First Trip to Remember

By Sarah Meadus

Our first trip into the Boundary Waters Canoe Area Wilderness was an adventure to remember. I've always loved camping and I've always loved storms, but experiencing both while in the middle of nowhere was a new, terrifying, experience. However, what doesn't kill you makes you stronger, right?

My husband and I had the worst tent in our group of five. It was a small, cheap model from a discount store. It had a miniscule rain fly. The "rain beanie," as I called it, barely covered the top of the tent – nowhere near long enough to reach the ground on all sides as a good rain fly should.

The third day of our July trip started with a light drizzle that continued the entire day. We caught some fish though, and had a delicious dinner. By then wind had picked up, it was still drizzling, and we could see lightning in the distance. A storm was rolling in.

Sometime after dark, as the lightning approached and we began hearing louder thunder, we decided to get into our tents and hunker down for the night. The rain had increased and the wind was blowing at a steady 20-30 m.p.h. I was terrified in our small, wet, inadequate tent. I could see the water pouring through the seams of the tent, creating puddles. I tried my best to move our clothing and gear to keep it somewhat dry. I was most worried that the rain beanie would blow away leaving us with nothing but the skimpy mesh tent top during a downpour.

I remember being scared out of my mind while trying to fall asleep. The wind was howling and we could hear the trees bending and swaying above us. It was blowing steadily, with gusts exceeding 50 m.p.h. Luckily, my husband was there for comfort. We snuggled into our sleeping bags, praying for the pitiful rain fly to hold as the wind tore at it.

Eventually, I feel asleep. The next thing I remember was my husband waking me up. He was up on his hands and knees and said "Get out of the tent." The rain was still coming down in sheets. I could hear the gusts of wind and feel the rumbles of thunder immediately following flashes of lightning. "No way!" I said, "I'm not going out there."

A little more forcefully he said, "I've got a tree on my back and I'm not sure how long I can hold it. Get out!"

That changed my mind. And that's when I noticed that his side of the tent had a lot less headroom. While I was sleeping, my husband had stayed awake to keep an eye and ear on things. After about 45 minutes, he heard the crack of a tree breaking. It sounded close. Really close. In a split second, he reacted. He got up on all fours bracing for possible impact. And he felt it. The crack had come from a tree right next to our tent. The trunk fell onto his back. That's when he woke me up to get out.

I quickly put on my coat to venture outside. My husband moved forward a little and found that while the tree was touching his back, he wasn't actually holding it up. Luckily, the tree base had snapped about three feet up from the ground. Our tent happened to be close enough to the trunk to fit into the triangle formed by the ground, the remaining trunk, and the cracked-off bulk of the tree. This saved our tent from being flattened and, better yet, saved us from being injured or killed.

We dragged our tent away from the downed tree. The storm was still raging and it was dark out, so there wasn't much we could do at that moment. We noted the tent poles didn't seem to be broken and the tent was still standing. It even looked like the collapsed side of the tent had popped up a bit. We climbed back into the relocated tent and hunkered down to wait for sunrise.

We awoke the next morning to gray skies and drizzle. The worst of the storm had passed. We later found out that there were 100 m.p.h. straight-line winds reported near us. We surveyed the damage and were amazed at how perfectly (and luckily) the tree landed on our tent without killing us.

If we'd pitched our tent a few feet further away from the tree trunk, the pine would have scored a direct hit. I was amazed the trunk had cracked like a matchstick. This was a live tree, probably a 75 feet tall. The wind broke it in an instant. Previous campers had cut all the lower limbs, branches, and twigs from the tree. It didn't occur to me until later how lucky it was that we avoided being stabbed by those branches.

We were able to use the tent for the final two days left of our trip, after which we immediately began a list of the new gear we wanted ... starting with a new tent.

# Lost on the Angleworm Trail

By Steve Gendron

In mid-April I could not contain my excitement for another paddling season in the Boundary Waters Canoe Area. Minneapolis was snow-less and warm, so I planned what I considered a "training trip" to hike the Angleworm Trail. Along on this trip was my 130-pound Alaskan Malemute, Andy.

I headed for the Boundary Waters on a mid-50-degree day with light sprinkles. By Hinckley, the temperature had dropped to the mid-40s, and the rain grew heavier. By Duluth and Two Harbors, it was low 30s and the rain had switched over to heavy, wet snow. Then, on to Ely, white knuckle driving, tense and anxious. Ely was a virtual "snow-globe."

Arriving at the trailhead, my pack was predictably swollen. A police officer friend had routinely advised me to carry a handgun on my solo hikes - "just in case." I had to decide between the gun and a birding book. As an English Literature major, the decision was easy.

The Angleworn is a 14-mile trail that starts just outside the Boundary Waters. The first several miles run generally west to east, often through swampy lowlands, occasionally intersected by creeks and ponds. Periodically, there is planking over the wettest sections. On this day the planking was several feet under water, including the open, flowing kind as well as ice. It was a mess, and we struggled with our hike. As the afternoon wore on, we reached the junction of the Angleworm and the Trease Lake portage. Nearby, there are several campsites, and we staggered, wet to the waist, to the closest one. I cooked rice over my campstove, and as evening darkened, ate and climbed into the tent.

The next morning, it was clear, becoming warm with spring breezes, and the previous day's snow was melting. Off we set, clock-wise around Angleworm, Home and Whiskey Jack lakes. I found a beautiful campsite above Angleworm. In a day, we had gone from a ravaging snow storm to early, warm spring. We had the woods to ourselves.

On our third day, I was excited to be a mere three or four miles from the car, and we broke our camp early, planning for a relaxed return hike to the trail head. After an hour, I became concerned. Our direction seemed off, and Angleworm Lake –

which should have been visible –was nowhere in sight. I suddenly realized we were lost!

For several hours we wandered, crossing slough ponds in a large circle, as lost people frequently do. At one point, I crossed an ice-covered wetland, and "crash," I was immediately chest-deep in water. Not only was it very cold, but it stunk of rotting duck weed and mucky decay. I changed clothes. I thought about the handgun I'd left in the car, which I could have used to signal rescuers. A gnawing panic flowed over me like a dark wave. Finally, buoyed by the sunshine, I studied the map and decided as long as I headed west, I would eventually find Angleworm lake.

Heading west, compass at the ready, I continued walking through the lowland swamp until I came to a 20-foot-wide creek. Was the ice safe? I took off my backpack and flung it across the ice. The ice held. On hands and knees, I inched across. If dogs can laugh, Andy probably was. He hesitatingly followed me. We then climbed a very steep hill, and found not only the trail, but the campsite which we had left eight hours before! We stopped and (again) pitched our tent there. That night, the rice and cheese supper had never tasted so good. The sun shone, the evening was beautiful, and the campfire was a relief.

In the morning, I chose the longer route back to the car, returning exactly the way we had come. I remained bewildered how we had gotten lost on the previous day. As we continued, near the Trease junction, Andy and I suddenly froze. Just ahead of us, 30 yards away, was a scantily clad woman. Was I now hallucinating? As it turned out, I was not. She wore only shorts and hiking boots. Not wanting to startle her, I coughed loudly She didn't seem the least disturbed. In fact, we talked for some time – I don't recall the topic – and then headed in our respective directions.

Shortly after that, I made it back to my car, which was another welcome sight.

# BWCA QUIZ #3

**1.)**  What is the Laurentian Divide?

**2.)**  When and where did the first logging operations take place in the BWCA?

**3.)**  How long does it take U.S. Forest Service personnel to dig a latrine pit at a designated campsite in the BWCA?

**4.)**  In addition to "the Root Beer Lady" Dorothy Molter, who was the other resident of the BWCA who was "grandfathered in" and allowed to live in the area following the enactment of the 1964 Wilderness Act?

**5.)**  How many packs did the French-Canadian Voyageurs typically carry over each portage? How heavy were the packs?

**BWCA Quiz #3 – Answers**

1.)  It's one of six Continental Divides in the U.S. The Laurentian Divide, sometimes called "the height of land," is a geographical formation that determines the flow of water. To the north of the divide, water flows northward to the Arctic Ocean. To the south of the divide, water flows southward toward the Gulf of Mexico, or, in some cases, east toward the Atlantic Ocean.

2.)  Records are scarce, but it is believed logging began in 1895 near Big Trout Lake, to the north of Lake Vermillion.

3.)  According to the U.S. Forest Service, it takes a two-person crew one to two hours to dig a latrine pit (depending on the location of the site and soil/rock conditions).

4.)  Benny Ambrose. After serving in World War I, Ambrose moved to the north country, eventually building a small cabin on Otter Track Lake. He lived there – working as a prospector, trapper and fishing guide – until his death in 1982.

5.)  The standard load for a voyageur was two packs, 90-pounds per pack, loaded with animal furs and / or other supplies.

# ANIMAL ADVENTURES

## A Season for Wilderness: The Journal of a Summer in Canoe Country *(Excerpt)*
By guest author Michael Furtman

*Michael Furtman is freelance writer and photographer special-izing in the outdoors. He is the author of many books, including* Magic on the Rocks: Canoe Country Pictographs, The New Boundary Waters Canoe Area and Quetico Fishing Guide, *and* Canoe Country Camping: Wilderness Skills for the Boundary Waters and Quetico. *The excerpts below, reprinted with Mi-chael's permission, are from his 1991 book* A Season for Wilder-ness: The Journal of a Summer in Canoe Country. *His books (signed by the author) and photographs can be viewed and pur-chased at www.michaelfurtman.com.*

Modern man may have lost many of the senses of his primitive ancestors, at least on a conscious level. There is one sense, however, that all of us can claim and that is the feeling of being watched. No doubt in more dangerous times this sense was vital.

As I began to untie the rope I hesitated uneasily. I was being watched. By whom or what, I had no idea, nor certainly where. I started to scan the area slowly and out of the growing shadows limed a blackness that was darker than its surroundings. Now that I had something to focus on I quickly identified the crea-ture. It was a bear.

I have read all the research that says that black bears are very rarely dangerous. Mostly black bears are shy but they can be big, opportunistic rascals, raiding campsites and scaring campers, showing just enough aggression to obtain food. Pests, yes; dangerous, rarely. That much I knew.

Face to face at 20 yards with a very, very large bear in a forest that was quickly growing dark, I realized that everything I had read seemed ridiculously trite. Darkness is the dominion of fear. Big animals, ones with lots of teeth and sharp claws, mix readily with that darkness to create an air of electricity. Which is why my hair was standing on end.

It occurred to me that this bear, seeing me lower a pack from a tree, would no doubt assume that it contained food. Hanging your food in a tree is a common way of protecting it from marauding black bears in the canoe country and because some campers are less adept at this technique than others, many bears have learned that this situation can lead to easy pickings. I had no doubt that this bear had dined on freeze dried lasagna in the past. It was almost dark. I needed to make a decision. I was tired and irritable and wanted that pack at least as much as the bear did.

"Hey Bear!" I screamed, "Get outta here."

The bear stood on its hind legs to better see over the meager brush that separated us. Doing so, he seemed to grow 10 times in size. I picked up a big stick.

"Gowan, get outa here!" I yelled again.

This time the bear took off as if a bee had stung its nose. It crashed downhill at a tremendous speed, going over and through the brush rather than around it. Then it stopped. It stopped in the darkness between me and the route back … completely out of sight in a heavy tangle of spruce and alder. The dark forest suddenly grew very still. Without the noise, I could only wonder whether the bear had simply stopped and was watching and waiting or had slipped quietly away. The silence was ominous.

It was dark now. I quickly lowered the pack, unwrapped it from the waterproof tarp, stowed the tarp in the pack and shouldered the load. And then with a tingle in my spine and a flutter in my heart, I lifted my voice in song and headed back…

I sang something to the tune of the "Yellow Rose of Texas" (I don't know why that song came to mind)… Silly perhaps, but the bear did let me through. I kept singing until I saw the light of the Coleman lantern…

# A Canoe Trip For The Birds

By Louise (Leoni) Thureen

It was spur of the moment planning. Pam knew I was anxious to get out into the woods for a few days, and she said rather casually: "You want to take a short canoe trip?"

"Yes!" was my immediate and unhesitating response.

There in Pam's small office at the *Ely Echo* newspaper (she was the paper's photographer), we set a date and began making our checklist of things to bring and buy.

I was busy getting ready, when a loud chirping sound brought me to a dead stop. My dad's cat had brought home a live baby robin. I was in charge of taking care of it, and it wanted to be fed. Who would dig for worms and feed it while I was gone, I thought?

My oldest boy and my daughter had summer jobs, and the other boys were too into summer fun to worry about feeding a bird. For one brief fraction of a moment I thought the trip would have to be cancelled.

With baby fluff still sticking out between newer feathers this bird was in no way ready to be turned loose. OK, I thought; he'll just have to make the trip with us ... and he did.

For the bird's food supply, a day's worth of worms was purchased at a bait shop and packed.

I prepared a plastic bucket and ventilated the cover as the bird's traveling basket. Stuffed with a soft rag and disposable paper towels on top of that, the bucket looked comfortable, and the holes in the lid were large enough for him to look through. I also packed a hand tool for digging more worms!

When Pam came to pick me up, I told her about the unexpected traveling companion, and she replied "Why not?" Now, THAT'S a real friend! The day was sunny, and just breezy enough to keep us cool. We had decided to paddle the whole length of Fall Lake.

As we paddled past motorboats, the robin was squawking so much I had to take him out of his little "home" and let him sit on my knee so he could see what was going on. We stopped paddling long enough for him to down a few worms. He seemed completely happy when I let him sit on the edge of his container-home, watching us paddle and looking around.

I fed him again; he'd already eaten a handful of worms as

we took rest breaks crossing the lake. The worm container was emptying faster than anticipated, so I looked around for a spot to dig for more worms. After some trial and error, we found that where there were dandelions, there would be worms in the roots. I packed more worms into his container.

We paddled on, portaged to Newton Lake, and checked the map for campsites. The robin once again claimed his view from my knee to direct our efforts and take in the sights.

Pam suggested a better name for the bird. She said he was such a good little bird he should have the name "Robingood." And so it was from then on.

Soon it was lunchtime again for Robingood. We dug up a few more worms ... even tried showing him where they came from, hoping he would get the idea. No luck. He just blithely chirped and hopped on down to the canoe as though he was ready for another ride.

We made camp, fished, and dug for still more worms. Time to turn in.

Robingood's basket was in the tent with us, but as the night grew colder, I worried it would be too cold for a baby robin with no mother or siblings to cuddle up to. So I put his basket in the sleeping bag with me, and we both went peacefully to sleep.

The next morning we packed up for our journey home. But Robingood discovered the water, and took his first bath. What a wretched looking little mite he was, all wet!

Our trip home was slow and easy, stopping to feed the ever-hungry Robingood from time to time. It had been a great, adventurous, wilderness journey of two friends ... and a baby robin.

POSTSCRIPT: Robingood grew up to be a beautiful bird. We taught him where to look for worms, and helped him learn to fly. When ready to be on his own, he took up residence in a tree near the house, and visited us often. He left in the fall, migrating to a warmer climate. In the spring, the beautiful song of a robin came from his favorite tree, and we all went out to look. I called out "Robingood!" and a gorgeous adult robin flew to the edge of the roof of our house, watching us and singing his song. He stayed about 20 minutes, then flew off to live his life. Tears of joy filled my eyes.

# Bear Knot
By Kim Johnson

A few years ago, three of us (my brother-in-law, Charlie, a friend, Bruce, and I) went on a canoe trip to the BWCA in the fall of the year. Charlie had a hunting license and brought along a shotgun to (hopefully) add grouse to the dinner pot. We set up camp on a snug site on Ensign Lake. The food pack was raised and securely tied with a double half-hitch knot to a conveniently located birch tree.

After dinner (without grouse) the campfire yarn-telling turned inevitably to bears. Vivid imaginations and cheap rum turned every night sound to that of ursine feet, claws, and teeth.

Suddenly one actually appeared in all its shaggy glory intent on the food pack hanging from the birch tree. At this point we headed to the tent. Charlie had his shotgun out and, at our collective urging, fired a shot into the air. The bear dropped to the ground and fled with the food pack firmly in its teeth.

A subsequent inspection showed that the hoisting rope had not been chewed through as we had suspected. Either the bear was amazingly dexterous or in the confusion of setting up camp, I must have tied a granny knot.

Later investigation showed a hidden cache of half a dozen Duluth packs, neatly shredded. The bears apparently made a practice of preying on passing canoeists' food packs to dine in style as well as the circumstances permitted.

# Solo Encounter
By Alex Needham

I had long dreamed of a solo trip to the BWCA.

One of my first tasks at camp was to hang the rigging for my food pack, 20 feet high, between two trees. My food was up, safe from bears, and I could rest easy.

After waking the next morning I decided to have oatmeal and tea, break camp and move on. I lowered my food pack and powered up my stove to boil water. There was no wind. Birds chirped and the sun shone. It seemed like a cheerful morning. I

didn't realize it when the birds stopped chirping and the squir-
rels stopped chattering and the forest became completely silent,
until I heard the thrashing in the woods behind me.

I looked over my shoulder and saw the top of a short spruce
shake violently some 60 feet to the left of camp. "Bear," I
thought, "And my pack is down and open!" I ran toward it. Then
I heard the dull, hollow stomping of hoof on earth. It was no
bear; it was a moose.

He trotted into camp halting on the trail behind the fire pit.
A bull moose, taller than a horse, at least half a ton, dark and
shining in the sun, stood 25 feet away below a giant spread of
antlers. The moose looked at my gear. His eyes moved to my
hissing stove on the rock before me. Then his eyes lifted to me.
I stared straight into them. For how long, I don't know.

I could hear two things: my heart pounding and my breath,
which were both too loud. I tried to slow my heartbeat with deep
long breaths. It was September and moose were in rut. "If he
charges me," I imagined, "one leap to the landing, and one dive
to the lake. One dive."

Slowly, deliberately, his head turned back toward the trail
and he trotted east as I exhaled, elated. Then I heard another
rustle in the trees. I saw two spruces start to bend and I realized
the moose had snagged the ropes of my food pack rigging with
his antlers. I heard the creak and twang of the rope pulling taut
(over 100 feet) and then a loud "SNAP" followed by a sound like
a laser burst. The trees sprang back upright.

There was an angry snort, a thrashing of antler on tree,
the sound of a tree snapping, and more stomping. The moose
was headed back toward me. By then I had retreated, and was
perched on a log hanging over the water. I crouched with my
shoulders almost between my knees. I wished I could vanish.
In seconds, I repeated my escape plan. "One leap to the rock," I
thought, "one dive to the water."

I heard him advancing quickly. Twelve feet from me he
stopped. I held my breath. I could see his antlers around the
cedar. Could he see me?

He stepped to the right and charged toward my tent. Near it he
hesitated and then ran down a trail into the woods. I listened as he
tore through the brush. Then, quickly, his sound vanished.

The rope, having snapped at its end near the moose's ear,

laid draped over his course down the trail. This was no clumsy beast. But in anger it pulled down a five-inch diameter spruce, its largest root snapped at the base. I still wonder whether a dive into the lake would have saved me if the moose was intent to thrash and stomp me.

The following night, a few lakes away, I lay in my tent listening to the sound of a moose bathing in a marsh, dipping into the water and draining its hide of gallons of rushing water. I'd sit up straight in the dark at the sound of nearing, accelerating footfalls only to realize them to be the sound of my blood pulsing through my ears.

## Bears Prefer the Uncola:
## A Lesson Learned the Hard Way
by Tom Cherveny

Long ago, the makers of 7-Up soda pop had the nerve to challenge the industry's goliath by calling it the "Uncola."

In the midst of that advertising campaign, we learned that bears indeed prefer the Uncola.

Our discovery came on one of our early Boundary Waters Canoe Area Wilderness trips.

We were cowered in our tent during a rain-filled night. It's when we least expected (or wanted) to make an important discovery of this nature. These days, we always set up our camp aware that we are in bear country. We take all the proper precautions. Food never enters our tent. We do dishes away from camp (and water), and likewise clean our fish nowhere near camp.

We firmly believe in the importance of hanging our food packs well out of reach.

But back in our learning years, we also liked to carry a couple of plastic bottles of soda pop on our trips. It was our treat for the first couple of days.

This particular trip started on Moose Lake, near Ely. We travelled all the way to Knife Lake and made a beeline for the nearest camp. Novices that we were to wilderness camping, it never occurred to us that there might be a reason why a camp so close to the Isle of Pines – home to the Root Beer Lady, Dorothy

Molter – would be vacant at the height of the summer season.

Dusk turned to night. We had the tent up and our most important job taken care of: A rope dangled over a limb, waiting to hoist our food pack at a moment's notice.

There was no notice when the dark sky above opened up and started pouring what seemed like the waters of Basswood Falls onto us. We pulled our food pack skyward. We dove into the tent like base runners racing a toss from the infield.

Not long after, we felt the swish of the bear that brushed against our tent.

We yelled, unzipped our tent door and probed the rain with our flashlights. My flashlight beam illuminated a problem. Maybe 15 or 20 feet from our tent stood a pair of plastic two-liter bottles of soda pop.

One was a bottle of Coca-Cola. And one was a bottle of 7-Up, newly re-branded as the "Uncola." We had forgotten to put them in the food pack for an elevator ride to the safety of the sky.

We banged two tin cups, shouted and howled and had some success in chasing our unwanted visitor away, only to have the bear return to camp, once again brushing past our tent.

This time the bear headed straight for the soda bottles. Our two flashlight beams were fixed on the bear like a performer in the circus. The bear proceeded to twist the 7-Up bottle like you would wring a towel to squeeze the water out. The intruder guzzled the carbonated sugar water.

Our bear never touched the dark-colored cola bottle. Did it blend too easily into the dark? Was it sealed too well for her to get a scent of the sugar water at her side?

We choose to believe the bear just preferred the Uncola.

We carried the twisted 7-Up bottle, with its distinctive bear tooth prints, home as a souvenir of a lesson learned.

## The Little Red Bandit
By Mike Subialka

On our group's annual trip into the BWCA, we make it a habit to pack one candy bar per person, per dinner. After we've finished our dinner, we take turns, one-by-one, selecting our favorite candy bar. Then we sit down and slowly savor our sweet dessert as the sun sets over the lake. It's our evening ritual.

But this story starts at breakfast.

I had just shoveled the last steaming spoonful of maple and brown sugar oatmeal into my mouth when the chattering started. It was a constant clicking, a cross between stern scolding and boastful taunting.

The tiny red squirrel blended almost perfectly with the bark of the red pine, but a flick of his tail proved he certainly wasn't afraid to let us know he was watching. The chattering grew louder and angrier as I started toward our food pack. I wanted to clean up the pile of food before this little rascal got any ideas about helping himself to his own meal.

It was the loose pile of sunflower seeds that caught my attention. They had spilled from the freshly chewed corner of the bag. CHATTER-CHATTER-CHATTER the squirrel said. Translation: "Ha-ha-ha, those sure were tasty!" That conniving little rodent must have snuck onto the tarp while we were huddled around the campfire enjoying our oatmeal. Not only did he hijack a half-bag of sunflower seeds, but he helped himself to about a dozen crackers as well. I packed the bag, tightly sealed the top, then raised it 10 feet off the ground. The battle was now over. Or was it?

A few hours later, on a hike back into the woods, I realized this wily red squirrel had pulled off a professional heist. In the middle of the trail was a full-size candy bar, half-eaten right through the wrapper. It had to be from our nightly dessert stash. CHATTER-CHATTER-CHATTER overhead. I gritted my teeth and continued down the trail. I soon found candy bar number two gnawed almost beyond recognition. CHATTER-CHATTER-CHATTER. I picked up the pace as I headed back to camp, wondering how many of our precious chocolate bars this little thief had nabbed. Every 50 to 100 feet there was another mangled reminder of that little red bandit. Twix, Three Musketeers, Milky Way and Hershey bars, all in various stages of nibbling. I picked up five mangled candy bars.

Back at camp, I dropped the food pack to assess the total damages. CHATTER-CHATTER-CHATTER. What we found was disheartening. In all, 13 of our 24 candy bars were missing. Throughout the week we discovered seven more of the missing bars scattered around the island. The remains of one candy bar (including wrapper) were never was discovered. CHATTER-CHATTER-CHATTER. Strangely enough, the Snickers bars we had packed, (advertised on all the major TV networks as "chock full of peanuts"), were left completely untouched in the pack. If you ask me, that's nuts! But if you ask that little red squirrel, I'm sure all you'll get is CHATTER-CHATTER-CHATTER.

## *A Bear Stole My Toothbrush*
By Jackie Bussjaeger

There were six of us campers and two counselors spending a week paddling the Boundary Waters. We arrived at an island campsite on Burnt Lake in the afternoon. We pitched camp, hung our food pack a distance away, and took a rest from our exhausting first day. One counselor began preparing dinner while the other provided a paddling lesson. Just as we had gathered, paddles in hand, we heard a loud thud.

Immediately, everyone stopped talking. We turned to face the direction of the noise. It had come from our food pack. Each of us thought same thing: we were about to face a wild bear.

A counselor hoisted her paddle and waved it around. She bellowed and sang loudy, advancing down the trail toward the food pack, yelling and singing. We all joined her. We stopped just short of where the bag was hung. I could see the pack, high above us, was swinging violently. It was rocking the same way a food bag would if an eight-foot-tall animal stood on its hind legs and pawed at it.

I thought, "WOW, it's BIG." There was a loud grunt as the bear noticed us and suddenly lunged. The counselor screamed "GO, GO, GO!" and six squealing campers and two terrified counselors charged back to the campsite. The food bag contained everything with any scent at all: mess kits, deodorant, lip balm, everything. The bear now had the bag and all it contained.

I thought, Mom will never believe me when I tell her a bear stole my toothbrush.

It was the best trip to the BWCA I've ever had.

# Grimace And Bear It

by Richard F. and Katherine K. Collman

It was 1970, two months after Katherine and I had been married in St. Cloud. In the sweltering heat of 94 degrees we headed north for the beauty of the BWCA and en route visited friends and their toddler on the Gunflint Trail. After a good overnight reunion with our friends, we headed to the end of the Gunflint Trail, then began paddling into Seagull Lake and toward Alpine and Jasper Lakes. Our goal was to overnight on a campsite on Jasper Lake.

We found a well-used site; a bit too well-used: bacon grease had been dumped by the fire pit. After a nice supper, we enjoyed the still evening. I was not feeling too well for reasons I didn't understand at the time. We headed to bed and sought sleep in stifling heat. Getting inside a sleeping bag was not even a consideration. It was too hot, even for clothes. Katherine tied the tent flaps open in desperate hope of some air circulation. As a precaution against bears, we had hung our food after supper. We took our bathroom kits and part of the cleaned up cook kit into the tent with us. Not a good idea.

By midnight my body was burning with fever (contracted from the sick child we had visited on the way up). Katherine, always restless in humid heat, lay awake. Smelling a heavy musky odor, Katherine said in a panicky loud whisper "Get your knife! I think there's a bear out there!"

"What? A bear?" I responded in a daze. Suddenly I heard a loud ripping as a gaping hole appeared from top to bottom in the back of our tent. "Make noise! Bang something, anything!" I ordered. We screamed and hollered and clapped our hands. Banging on the cook kit, we sounded an alarm that would have awakened anyone across the lake. We heard the bear run off.

With hearts beating in panic and a full moon illuminating the scene, we tried to decide what to do. Run - where? Move - where? Stay and chance a revisit by Mr. Bear?

By now my body was feverish and my head pounded. We threw on clothes, tossed the sleeping bags into the canoe, and started to paddle out to a small island. The island had a a few places to lay out our sleeping bags. I think my feverish state put me back into some kind of slumber. Katherine lay awake with all senses on alert. We hoped this bear didn't swim! Grimace and bear it.

The sun could not rise quickly enough. When morning light came, I was weak but the fever had broken. We paddled back to our campsite. We took our food down, packed up as quickly as possible, folded up our now air-conditioned tent, and started to paddle out. By the time we put our canoe in the water, Katherine was feverish and unable to do much paddling and no lifting. Seagull Lake was hot and still. I paddled both of us out as best I could. I can't even remember the portages.

We got to the the Gunflint Trail, located our car, and drove to the first motel we came across. We slept 17 hours straight.

## Close Encounter [or No S@#t!]
By Susan Jane Cheney

My closest, most unusual experience with the stodgy "woodchuck – or "groundhog," as it is sometimes called – occurred several years ago in the BWCA. It was May, and we went in at the Poplar Lake Entry Point. Near the end of our week-long trip, we were camped on Horseshoe Lake.

After dinner, I ambled up the wooded trail to the latrine. As fellow BWCA trippers know, this is nothing more than an open-air overturned "box" with a hole in the surface. It is situated on the ground in a small clearing some distance from the fire grate at each campsite.

Not long after I was seated, I was startled to see a silvery brown head pop out of a hole in the ground near the base of the box. The eyes were pointed away from me. Soon, the rest of the animal, a plump, mature woodchuck, emerged and sat almost completely still, intently focused on the woodland setting and subtle evening sounds.

The top of the sleek, smooth head was just inches from my right shin; I could have easily lowered my hand and stroked the fur with my fingertips. Barely breathing in amazement, I simply watched, waiting to see what would happen. The woodchuck sat, small perked ears occasionally twitching, for several minutes and then dashed forward. Without a backward glance, it disappeared into the low vegetation among the trees, apparently totally unaware of its close encounter with me.

# Rare Sighting in May

By Susan Jane Cheney

On a cool, overcast and misty early May morning, my older brother, husband and I were making our way north on long, narrow Heritage Lake in our solo canoes. I was in the lead, the two men lagging a bit behind, paddling next to one another and engaged in conversation. Rhythmically manipulating my double paddle, I carefully studied the shoreline on either side watching for any signs of wildlife – so rarely seen in the BWCA because of their natural camouflage and ease of hiding. Still, the chance of spotting something seemed more likely at this time of year – just after "ice out" when trees had not yet leafed out and the ground vegetation was sparse, affording better sightlines into the woods and at the water's edge.

We passed one of the lake's campsites, situated high up on the west side, then paddled past a second site where the lake narrowed considerably. Not long after that point, I spied move- ment on the left shore; a large cat-like animal was methodically wending its way over and around the rocks just above the wa- terline heading in the same direction as we were. Its long thick tail stretched out behind its sinuous body, and I knew it was a cougar rather than its shorter-tailed lynx or bobcat cousins.

Several days later, when we came out and were enjoying our usual post-trip layover in Ely, we heard that a few rare cougar sightings had been reported in the area that spring – a fact that local merchants were not eager to broadcast, reasoning that campers might be scared off by the presence of these predatory wild creatures. Personally, this cat lover was thrilled by my first large feline sighting in the BWCA.

# FROM THE HEART

## *The Big Circle*
By guest author Sam Cook

*Sam Cook is a longtime columnist for the* Duluth News Tribune
*and the author of a series of books that evoke the spirit of the
woods and waters of the North Woods. His books include* Moving
Waters: Adventures on Northern Rivers, Quiet Magic, Friendship Fires, *and* Up North, *from which this essay is reprinted with
Sam's permission. Sam's blog,* Outdoors with Sam Cook, *can be
found at samcook.areavoices.com.*

We met the two men on one of the portages leading to Knife
Lake. We were on our way into the woods for a week. They were
on their way home.

What I remember best is the cooler those two men were
carrying. They opened it and showed us the fish they'd caught in
Knife, the biggest lake trout I'd ever seen.

My wife and I were making our first trip together into the
border country. We were green to the ways of the woods then,
and, to be honest, a little apprehensive.

It was reassuring to meet a couple of woodsmen who seemed
so comfortable, so at home. They were from Duluth, they said.
They came up as many weekends as they could, always to fish
lake trout. They were portaging a square-stern canoe and motor.

"We can leave Duluth and be on Knife in six hours," one of
them said.

After we'd chatted for a while, I got up enough nerve to ask
the men for a favor. Phyllis and I had been outfitted for our trip

by an Ely outfitter. We'd stopped for lunch to look through our packs to see if we had everything we needed. We had found no rope. We would need some if we were going to hang our food pack and keep it away from the bears.

I told the men our problem and asked them if they had some rope they could spare. They didn't hesitate. One of them dug into a worn Duluth pack and pulled out two hunks of rope.

I was a little embarrassed asking for the rope. It wasn't like we were borrowing it. I knew we'd never see the men again. They knew it too. But they gladly gave us all we needed.

We chatted a little more, then went our opposite ways down the portage.

I guess that was one of the first times I found myself part of the Big Circle. Back then I had no conception of what the Big Circle was. In fact, I'd never heard it called that until a few summers ago when a bush pilot at an Indian village in northern Manitoba referred to it. The pilot had opened his home to us that afternoon, prepared us lunch, and let us take a shower. We tried to thank him and asked how we could repay him.

"Forget it," he said. "You'll do someone else a favor sometime. It's all part of the Big Circle."

I liked the concept. Because of the nature of bush travel, you often can't repay those who help you. But you can help somebody else, somewhere down the trail.

Sooner or later, it all comes around again. That's the Big Circle.

Phyllis and I have never again seen those two men who gave us the rope that day on the portage. But a few years later ... we showed a couple from Colorado some good spots to camp and fish. It was their first trip to the canoe country and they appreciated the information.

I didn't think anything of (the Big Circle) when three of us opened our campsite to a couple of weary women on the Kekekabic trail one September, either. But then, there I was the next summer in a remote Manitoba Indian village, eating a lunch served by a bush pilot I'd met just a few hours earlier.

One summer Mike Furtman and I stopped at a restaurant in Two Harbors for breakfast on our way up to do some fishing in the Boundary Waters Canoe Area Wilderness. Furtman had just written a booked called *A Boundary Waters Fishing Guide*.

The couple in the next booth were dressed as if they, too,

were headed for the woods. The man leaned over our booth and said, "Excuse me, but do you guys know anything about fishing in the Boundary Waters?"

Furtman and I looked and each other, then smiled. We spent the next several minutes recommending a lake, drawing a map of it on a napkin, and talking about how to catch smallmouth bass.

We felt good. Probably about as good as a couple of Duluth men felt 10 years ago when they gave those greenhorn paddlers the rope they needed.

 **OVERALL BEST ESSAY,** B WC A Reader, Volume 1

## *In Those Moments*
By Lee Vue

*Lee Vue's essay was judged the best overall essay for the* BWCA Reader, Volume 1. *Lee was presented a $250 check for her work. Lee, now 23, holds a Bachelor of Arts degree in Political Science from the University of Minnesota. She continues to visit the BWCA each year, and she continues to have wet feet on each visit.*

At 13, I was filled with self-doubts and straddling between two worlds: Hmong old traditions and modern expectations of the American Dream. It was an age of momentous discoveries that included boys, the natural process of my changing body, the pressure of future educational endeavors, and forming friendships among lost souls in crowded high school hallways. I had spent my entire life in an urban setting. Who knew a world of fantastical imagery of lakes and forests existed beyond the bounds of the city thriving on technology obsession?

If one small step for man on the moon was a giant leap for mankind, then my nervous first step onto the soil of the BWCA was the premonition of the woman I would become. The air had never felt so fresh. I wished I could breathe through my pores. The ground beneath me was firm, rooted with reminiscences of explorers from centuries before. But my knees were trembling from the undercurrents of wanting to go home because every-thing around me was foreign and unknown. Even if I wanted to run back to the security of a summer routine sitting in front of the television, home was six hours away. That feeling in the pit of your stomach when you're standing in front of a crowd was making my skin crawl with anticipation. I was embarking on a journey unknown in the life I had lived until this moment. It was as if a needle was about to burst my comfort bubble. Excitement and fear seethed together within me as I struggled to put things into perspective. Here I was, hundreds of miles away from home, entrenched in the BWCA, spending a week of my summer at YMCA Camp Menogyn to do the outrageous: camping, canoeing and portaging.

One camp counselor (Mo), one chaperone (Kao), seven teenage girls, and three canoes set out into the wild. Due to our poor canoeing abilities, we had to battle the headwind across West Bearskin Lake while occasionally struggling with the branches along the shoreline. In hindsight, this indicated that frustration and challenges were bound to ensue on the trip. Through a disastrous start, we gained a hard-earned understanding of the appropriate ways to canoe. We felt strained enthusiasm, and unexpected weariness.

In the quiet mornings when the lakes were calm and the only noise echoing through the trees was birds chirping, I often awoke with the single thought dancing through my mind: the dreadful deed of putting on wet socks and boots. It was insufferable, the ordeal of constantly wet feet in order to endure another day in the great outdoors. There was nothing enjoyable about the cold and damp feeling of soggy boots as I struggled to embrace the morning routine of packing up and venturing to the next campsite.

If wet boots weren't enough to sour my morning mood, portaging throughout the day made me sigh with a joyless expression. Every time we approached the start of a portage, my heart dropped. Portaging was the villain in my grand BWCA undertaking. The whole concept of carrying your packs and canoes across the connecting land to the next lake was preposterous and hard labor. My teammates and I had conceived a plan to ensure that we would all work together to lessen the load. We designated three people to carry one canoe and two people to a Duluth pack. Portaging often took us hours because we failed to realize that carrying one canoe only required one person and Duluth packs weren't going to break our backs. Mo and Kao never interfered with our learning process and allowed us to make the mistake. I think they secretly laughed at the absurdity of seven girls portaging the way we did. It was on the very last day that we took the risk of allowing one person to carry the canoe. I was the first person to volunteer. Yes, volunteer. Why? I'm not sure why I took the initiative. I'm not one to step up; my comfort level is more about moving myself to the back and observing. Something inside urged me to raise my hand. The tension was building, rising from the tingles of my feet to my fingertips. I felt as though as I was being electrocuted as my hand shot up into the air with a need to be THE ONE to carry the canoe. As we propped the canoe onto my shoulders, I was so afraid that I would falter, afraid the canoe would get damaged. But a small voice inside me chanted over and over, "You can do it!"

At that point in my life, I didn't have much belief in my own abilities, especially in a world where you're constantly compared to others and your worth is measured by your merits. I had no merits. I had no unique skill. I was simply "just myself," an extremely quiet Hmong girl who accepted her place in society. Oddly enough, the first step became two, three, a dozen, and then hundreds. When I reached the end of the portage and the canoe was safely in the water, I had never felt so proud of myself. My spirit soared with adrenaline and satisfaction. I did it!

Suddenly, time was ticking by too quickly as our laughter glided across the lake. We recalled our inexperienced and inelegant portaging technique. That seemed like ages ago now that we were true portagers. The morning we arrived back at Camp Menogyn, there was an unspoken yearning in my eyes. I wanted to remain in the BWCA a little longer. Another day. Maybe two. I wanted to remedy my initial reactions to the BWCA and everything it had to offer. In those few precious seconds as the bus was rolling down the dirt road toward civilization, a deep sensation of a great loss overcame me. It was in that moment, not a few minutes before or after, that I missed all that I had earlier dreaded: raging paddling wars with the wild winds on the chaotic waves of the lake, portaging through muddy and overgrown trails, the cringing feel of wet boots on my feet. Instead, my mind was filled with pleasurable recollections: watching the sunset as I devoured mac and cheese, waking up to the peaceful sound of stillness, hearing the loons as I snuggled into my sleeping bag, filling my vision at the wonderment of the stars above, fulfilling the challenge of carrying a heavy canoe on my shoulders, and the satisfaction of knowing that I was courageous enough to do something I had thought myself unable to.

Something deep within me had shifted. It was profound and awe-inspiring. I knew I was not the same girl whose first step was filled with hesitation and apprehension. The spark inside me was burning to become the person I was within the wildness of the BWCA: strong-willed, self-assured, determined, and enlightened with the intense knowledge of who I was – who I am. Perhaps, I wanted to prove to my parents I was more than the expected role of what a Hmong daughter should be. Perhaps I wanted to prove to society that I wasn't as timid and shy as they thought. Perhaps I wanted to prove to my teammates that I was as strong as they were. Most importantly, I wanted to prove to myself that the limitations and expectations placed on me by others did not determine who I was. Only in the transformative BWCA did I come to understand the insight of who I am, my soul, and passion.

## My Child, Up North
By Lindsey Dyer

I brought a baby to the Boundary Waters Canoe Area.

When I say "baby," I don't mean a laughing, chubby cherub with a two-toothed grin. I mean an infant, blind to her surroundings, except her mother's chest. She was six days old when she traveled up, a trip that would mark her unique beginning in this world. I named her Maria, and she held all of the hope of a first-born child.

I wanted her to be like a little seed in the wilderness, nestled in the brush. I wanted myself to be polished by wind and soil and friendly critters who would return me to the world anew. I would grow my little child like the earth would grow me, and I would be her shelter.

We stayed in a weathered log cabin, 20 feet from the shore of Burntside Lake. I nursed her by the window. We would rock as I watched the quiet waves. Little songs would be whispered as

Maria slept in my lap. For the first time in years, perhaps for the first time in my entire adult life, I didn't have television. There was no Internet, no social media. Fitting, as I made room for my one true charge – keep this little soul now in my care alive.

I would nestle her into my sling, wrapped around my shoulders and stretched across my back. She would bounce as I walked the trails and dirt roads, always silent. Pine scent filled the air, and my lungs grew strong with the medicine. My baby loved the air, and I think the North Woods air loved to flow into her as well. The cold mornings flushed her cheeks, and I would cover her from the chill.

When her umbilical cord fell off, we planted it in a small mound of dirt. I like to think the green that grows from that soil will breathe Maria. Her tiny whisper will speak to the new growth that surrounds her.

On the 4th of July, I brought her out at night, much past her baby bedtime. She was bundled tight in her green fleece wrap and strawberry hat. Her little beaded eyes watched the sky. I wondered how close she felt to that other world. Did she see what I saw? Maria looked on, concentrating on Orion, the Big and Little Dipper.

Burntside Lake was a steady friend that summer. There are a million ways to describe its water - but I tell you this, it knew me. It called to me. At night, I would pour a single cup of coffee and head down to the dock. Sitting cross-legged near the edge, I would be inspired by the stars and the water and the unchanging islands. Feeling free from the walls of city life, I didn't look back. With baby asleep not inside me, but behind me in the quiet cabin, I felt my new world unfolding, my world as a mother.

I would think about the women who gave birth up north, without an anesthesiologist, or perhaps even those who lived too far away from the reach of doctors or the hospital. They gave birth at home, naturally, in pain or not. In the end, their babies' lungs would burst into life, filled with the crisp boundary waters air, a clean and fresh air ready to fuel a baby's cry.

On our last day in the BWCA, we dipped her toes in the water. She wailed as Burntside Lake kissed her tiny two-month feet. We packed the car and headed back to St. Paul. I was anxious and hesitant.

I wondered if I would have been better off in the Cities after

Maria was born, mothers and friends and help readily at hand. I might have fared better. Maybe I wouldn't have felt so alone. Then, I start to think about what I would miss. The cool north air turning my child's fresh cheeks a shade of pink. The look on her face, peeking out of her tightly fastened fleece wrap, viewing her new universe. And my quiet conversations with the stars. And in those moments, when you feel a part of something and answers enter your heart, being alone can be okay.

## *An Unexpected Evening Serenade*
By Greg Hedlund

I was on my longest BWCA backpacking trip ever, finishing my two-week adventure on the Kekekabic trail.

I had seen no one the entire time. As I settled into a campsite next to Snowbank Lake for my last night, I felt sad and a little depressed. But I had a great site looking across a large bay. I anticipated my view of a beautiful sun set.

As I sat there I saw two canoes coming across the lake. Loud disturbing voices were an obnoxious noise that I hadn't heard in two weeks. They also had a boom box blasting music in the canoe! Civilization was greeting me. The canoes came closer and I hoped against hope they would pass the nearby campsite and go on to the next portage. No such luck. They turned to the left of me and the party kept going.

I was about to confront the party animals when the music stopped, I figured they were getting ready for dinner; this was likely just a short break.

About 30 minutes passed and I saw two young men get into their canoe for what I assumed would be a tip-and-dip and the obnoxious party would start all over again.

Was I wrong! The young man at the bow took out a violin and started playing the most moving and peaceful music the BWCA had ever heard. Even the animal life seemed to be in synch with it. He serenaded as the sun set. Sometimes on quiet nights, I can still hear that music.

# "If You're Travelin' in the North Country Fair…"

By Pete LaFave

My love affair with the BWCA started when I was 13 years old. I signed up for a week-long paddle through an Ely-based wilderness camp. There were four boys and two counselors who certainly had their hands full. We boys had never canoed before, or slept in a tent. It was as if our parents had read some universal recipe book: *Take four pubescent boys, place in wilderness, add mosquito bites, wind and rain, allow seven days to be fully sun-baked, remove after last portage. Enjoy!*

I vividly remember the first day. Our journey began from the Fernberg boat launch on Snowbank Lake. This big lake can be windy, making it a difficult introduction to the BWCA for beginners. You could tell we were newbies from a mile away. We steered exaggerated zig-zags, and a guy in the bow was using his bent shaft backwards. Needless to say, it absolutely poured that night, soaking our tent, sleeping bags, personal belongings, and our souls. We survived, but as we pushed out into the waters the next morning, some of us wondered if we should've signed up for that soccer camp instead.

All the boys wanted to gain acceptance from each other in our superficial 13-year-old ways. We wanted to be cool and to fit in. The last thing we wanted to do was admit the wondrous beauty in nature, or reveal any emotions about how this place affected our souls. Conversations remained centered around safe 13-year-old boy stuff. Yet the magic of woods and water soon crept in. Things began to change.

We laughed and whooped for joy when the waves tossed us, hung on every word from our wise and god-like counselors, and proudly showed off our blistered palms at the day's end. The defining moment of the entire trip occurred on the fourth day. After a long paddle the day before, it was decided that a layover day was in order. That morning was quiet, overcast, and cold. We had just finished pancakes when our counselor sprung his brilliant plan on us.

"You know what this morning needs?" he smiled whimsically, "How 'bout a silent, meditative paddle?" He was sure to emphasize the *silent* and *meditative* part. "Is this mandatory, Captain Fun-Hater?" asked the resident smart-aleck. "Excellent question! That's something you can contemplate out on the water," the counselor said as he handed him a paddle. We were all laughs as we pushed out into the cold, calm grayness of Kekekabic.

Soon we were hushed. The lake was so still. So perfect. As I found the rhythm in my paddle strokes, my mind wandered, my thoughts flowed through the calm. Family, friends, God, school, the girl I liked back home, the world, the universe. I was enveloped in my thoughts, quietly watching my counselor paddle in the bow, and the whirlpools flowing from his strokes. "So, whatchya been thinking about?" he finally broke the silence. "Everything," was all I could say. "I love it here." "That's the truth," he responded softly. We talked about this place, these mystical waters, the people who inhabited this place for thousands of years, leaving no trace except simple, red-ochre illustrations on the rocks. "Can you imagine if it wasn't the wilderness it is now?" he asked. "Can you picture buildings, boats, and noise all along these shores?" For the first time I grasped what this place really is, and why it needed to stay this way.

In varying degrees all members of the group had similar experiences that day. That night in the tent we talked about one kid's anxiety over starting high school that fall. Another revealed struggles over his parents' divorce. Real issues and real emotions.

I have returned to the North Country every year since. Every summer I escape. It's good for me. I live near Los Angeles, where it's hot, crowded, and dusty. Sometimes when I see the smoggy orange glow in the night sky, I pretend that it's the northern lights, and I wait for summer, when I can sit on a large slab of granite, smell the pines, and listen to the waves lap against the rocks. When I have kids, I'll take them there. Maybe we'll take joy in the portages, bugs, rain, and dehydrated food. Maybe – no definitely – on our layover day I'll say, *"How 'bout a silent, meditative paddle?"*


## Strength of the Spirit
By Mary Ann Schultz


On my first BWCA trip, I realized that I was not cut out for this rugged activity. I'm five-foot-two, and was never athletic.

My college-age group prided themselves in hauling all canoes and packs in one trip across the portages, some up to a mile long. This meant that I had to double-pack with a 30-pound pack on the front and a 40-pound pack on my back. If there was a fallen tree on the trail, I physically could not lift my leg to step over it because the front pack hung down to my knees, preventing me from flexing at the hip. Often on long portages I simply had to take off the packs and rest. I was mosquito-bitten, sore and exhausted. I was humiliated when others from the group who made it to the end of the portage had to come back and take my share of the load.

Also, our trip leader was used to bossing high school kids and was treating her fellow college students the same way. She would bark orders and want them executed immediately, if not sooner.

Morale was low, when several days in we approached our last portage of the day. There were three empty canoes pulled up along the bank but no people in sight. Our group assumed the party was making two trips to haul their equipment. Since I was the slowest and weakest, I got loaded up to head down the portage before everyone else. The trail was steep and rocky and swarming with mosquitos. If I could have quit and gone home, I would have. Just as I was feeling my lowest and most sorry for myself, I looked up and could not believe what I saw. Ahead of me on the trail was a young man, attempting to propel himself across the rocky terrain in a wheelchair. He was giving instructions to another man who was pushing the wheelchair from behind. It became apparent that the second man was visually challenged. Some other adults with them acknowledged my approach and made space for me to go around their party. They shared that they were a group out of Minneapolis (which later became Wilderness Inquiry). Their goal was to prove that wilderness could be accessible for anyone. They worked as a team and provided modifications for impairments but each individual was expected to contribute in whatever way he or she could.

I asked how they got the wheelchair into the canoe. When the canoe was put into the water, they explained, they carried the wheelchair user to the canoe and lowered him (or her) in. Next, they folded up the wheelchair and added it to the canoe. They further explained that the man – a paraplegic – had amazing upper body strength and was one of their strongest paddlers.

He needed only a modified canoe seat with back and side supports to stabilize him. The person with the visual challenges said he could handle any camping task as long as someone provided guidance. He'd been to the BWCA as a teen was recalling the smell of pine and the sounds of the canoe swishing across the water.

By now my group had caught up, so we wished our new friends well and continued to the end of the trail. Before us was a challenge no one expected. To reach open water and set the canoes down we would have to wade about 15 feet through thick mud. With each step I was afraid of losing my boots. I had to have a boost from one of the taller canoists to get unstuck and over the side of the canoe. I imagined the struggle to come for the group behind us.

The mood of our trip then changed. The bickering stopped. The pace became more relaxed. I know we were all doing a lot of thinking. I quit feeling sorry for myself and realized how grateful I was for the abilities that I possessed. I now saw beauty of a different kind, beauty that I was too inwardly focused to see before. The wilderness had much to teach about how strength of the spirit is often our biggest ally.

Author's note: For more information about Wilderness Inquiry, go to www.wildernessinquiry.org

## White Otters
By Dan Roettger

I starved myself for four solid days before loading the canoe and heading for the BWCA.

Once in, I spent the next six days continuing my fast without consuming so much as a granola bar. I worked hard every day, dumping in and out of an average of five lakes before setting myself up on a boulder each night, cross-legged, overlooking a different picture-perfect lake, and firing up a fresh ceremonial cigar.

I had no real idea how to go about a vision quest, but I wanted something to happen. If a hunger-induced, every-neuron-firing-moment of intense clarity was what I got, then fine.

If a white otter swam up to me on my rock, flipped over onto his back and calmly told me my real name was *gichi-ogimaa* (Ojibwe for "the highest leader") and I would soon be called on to pursue my higher purpose, all the better.

Alone in the wilderness, going on 10 days without food, my first revelation was that I was not at all hungry, and in fact felt perfectly normal. I had finally reached my target lake, a huge body of water even by BWCA standards. After quickly setting up camp I hustled back to my empty canoe, grabbed a 30-pound rock I called Igneous (which later became "Ig," my constant companion), placed it up front in the canoe and fished. In less than half an hour the BWCA gave up a revelation: lake trout will bite nonstop when they know you won't be eating them. I started out putting a scratch into the side of my canoe for every fish I caught, but stopped when it seemed I'd run out of canoe.

## Silence on the Kiwishiwi
By Al Zdon

The first few snowflakes drifted down just as we entered Lake One. It was later than our usual trip to the Boundary Waters. I had been lamenting my group's inability to coordinate schedules when my friend John called.

Why don't we just go up? John suggested. Indeed, why not? It was a little late, but I've chipped ice out of my fishing reel more than once in past years. So there we were, cramming gear into the canoe in late October. We headed out, and few more flakes blew our way as we paddled south. A couple of short portages and a moderate paddle later, we were at our favorite campsite on the South Kiwishiwi.

We got our tent set up, unloaded the gear, ate lunch and scavenged a little firewood.

I could probably hang around the camp for eternity, but John is an enthusiastic fisherman. So, we headed out.

We were on the river, just a few hundred yards from our camp, when another snowflake came down. And then two, and then a dozen. The water was absolutely still, not a ripple.

Pretty soon it was coming down with some authority, and

then we couldn't see the shoreline anymore. That's unusual, especially on a river where the shoreline is typically close at hand and very visible.

Then it really started snowing. The visibility shrunk to a few score yards, then maybe 10 yards, and then to an area no bigger than the length of the canoe.

I turned around and looked at John, but there was nothing to say. We just smiled at each other.

One of the reasons people go to the Boundary Waters is for the quiet. No city noise, no highway noise, no barking dogs, no whining lawn mowers. For those few minutes in the middle of that snow cascade, though, the quietness took on an almost mystical, spiritual quality.

There was no sound. We were in a little white world that nothing could penetrate. There was just the canoe, the water and us.

It took a few minutes, it took an eternity. Then, just perceptibly, the snow squall began to lift. Portions of the river began to reappear. Eventually, a dim shoreline could be seen.

And then it stopped snowing.

In four decades of paddling, I've had some amazing experiences – encounters with moose and bear, hearing a pack of wolves howling when I was alone on an island, times around the campfire when the singing was like a heavenly chorus.

But none of those stories really compares to those few minutes in late October when nothing at all happened – except the silence.


## Wall-Eyed
By Corey Eastwood

*"At this point the ferocious inwardness of the pain produced an immense distraction that prevented my articulating words beyond a hoarse murmur; I sensed myself turning wall-eyed, monosyllabic..."*
    - From William Styron's "A Darkness Visible"

When I was a child, my pediatrician diagnosed me with an abnormally low standing body temperature; a good two degrees under 98.6. As far as I know – aside from jabbing me full of vaccines – he never tested my capacity to tolerate pain. It wasn't until years later, during a period of youthful poverty when my employment consisted of selling plasma once or twice a month and submitting myself to medical experiments at the local university, that I received a "pain vigilance" exam. The test was rather straightforward. They secured a current to my pointer finger and shocked me. It began as a tingle in my finger, then, after getting my assurance that I could handle more, they cranked up the voltage so that the electric jolt extended to my knuckle, then to the rest of my hand. I suppressed my grimace and told them to go on until the pain reached my elbow and concerns of a heart attack or loss of the limb won over my desire to prove my masculinity. When giving me my envelope with $25 inside, the technicians thanked me and said I'd scored higher than average. I relate these pieces of medical history because they are important in explaining my May 2011 trip to the Boundary Waters.

All my life I'd heard about the BWCA from my Minnesotan uncle. He sent me a BWCA map that, to this day, hangs in my childhood bedroom. He regaled me with tales of five-foot walleyes, bear attacks and the most pristine wilderness left on the continent. I'd spent years in New York City, dreaming about visiting the BWCA. Finally, at age 30, my uncle and his longtime friend, Bill, invited me and my father to join them on their annual spring trip.

We flew out of La Guardia. My mother told me she'd put some extra clothes for me in my Dad's luggage in case I hadn't packed warmly enough. While not an expert camper, I'd spent my fair share of nights outdoors, and given my low body temperature, I knew that layers were a must. So, while it was a nice gesture, I told her it was unnecessary. I had packed the proper amount of clothes.

In my uncle's living room outside of Minneapolis, as we laid out our gear in three monstrous Duluth packs, I began to worry that maybe I wasn't as prepared as I'd thought. My uncle, a lifelong Minnesotan who's always struck me as impervious to the cold, looked at our meager clothing piles and went upstairs to round up more layers. He returned with a few pairs of oversize wool trousers and a synthetic sweater. My father declined the pants saying they'd get in the way during our long portages. I accepted both offerings, but feared they were a portent of frigid things to come.

Our first night, spent in an outfitter's bunkhouse on the outskirts of the Boundary Waters, wasn't completely insufferable. There was no heat, but the walls sheltered us from the wind coming off the lakes. We had a few beers and listened to loons bleat their intergalactic lullabies before I bundled up in my sleeping bag.

The next day we paddled and portaged. While my uncle is an experienced woodsman, we could not have possibly had a finer guide than Bill. An architect in his early 50s, Bill is to the Boundary Waters what Crocodile Dundee is to the Outback. Within minutes of meeting him, as he quadruple-checked both his packing list and the one he'd made for us, I could see he had decades of trips under his belt. As we dipped the bows of our canoes into the crisp BWCA water and pushed off, I felt confident I was in very good hands.

Lugging the 60-pound Duluth bags and the equally heavy and cumbersome canoes was not an easy task. Yet my uncle, who'd recently had hip surgery, appeared to be getting on fine carrying his canoe. Bill seemed to actively enjoy the work; each time I looked back, scowling with exhaustion as the muscles in my back ripped like threads of a rope, he was whistling, donning the exultant smile of a monk. It was my father and I, the hearty Yankees, both trying to out-macho one another, who struggled over the jagged roots, loose rocks and puddles of the portages. As arduous and somewhat painful as that aspect of the trip was, I'd rather have spent all four days doing nothing but portaging and paddling than endure a minute of what was to come that night.

We arrived at a small island to waning daylight and calls from the evening's first loons. Canoes ashore, we got to work setting up camp. This effort consisted mostly of the three of us playing with poles and knots while Bill turned camping into poetry; raising the tents on just the right surface, securing a the bear-proof food rig high in a tree and building a weather-versatile kitchen canopy next to the fire pit. When everything was set, my uncle asked if we wanted to go fishing. While I would happily eat a fish, I wanted nothing to do with going out in a boat or standing near the shore. It was freezing – literally – and I had only three desires: the hot jambalaya Bill was preparing, the warm whiskey I'd wisely procured at the last liquor store in town, and my sleeping bag. The extra warm one.

As I sat, covered in blankets and straddling the fire, my father and uncle chided me for being a wimp. The temperature felt like it'd dropped 25 degrees with the sunset and the cold was all I could talk about; pain was slowly becoming my entire sentience. In my 30 years I'd endured illness, squalor and a variety of other hardships. And while I'd scored well on my pain vigilance exam, they were absolutely right; when it came to the cold, I was a wimp. As we sat passing the bottle and fantasizing about the fish we'd catch the next day, I saw myself transforming from one of the gang, talking, laughing and functioning, into some sort of subhuman creature existing almost entirely in survival mode.

The pain Styron refers to in the epigraph to this essay is a mental one – clinical depression – and though the pain I experienced from the Boundary Water cold was primarily physical, it bled indistinguishably into my psyche; a fully integrated miasma. Looking around the campsite at fire-lit faces grinning, laughing, and growing increasingly blurry, I wondered if I were hallucinating or just experiencing my last breaths of life; the strobe light at the end of the tunnel.

I spent the night in my sleeping bag willing myself not to die while watching my water bottle freeze. As the first vestiges of dawn began to glow through the tent, I was tormented by false hope. Getting up offered the promise of hot coffee, a new fire or perhaps some old embers, but it also required leaving my sleeping bag. No one else was awake and I was convinced Bill was too prudent a camper to leave the fire smoldering. I spent another few hours lying there looking at the frozen water bottle.

So this was the Boundary Waters? This was the experience I'd been anticipating with such enthusiasm for so many years? I thought of the places I would rather be at that moment. I'd rather be arriving at middle school, on a day when I hadn't studied for any of my exams, where eager gauntlets of bullies were well-primed to extract blood. I'd rather be in jail unsure of when I would be getting out so that each moment of hope is also one of extreme torture. Hell, come to think of it, I might rather be tortured, so long as that torture chamber wasn't freezing! Instead of picturing a sunny beach, I took comfort imagining warm torture chambers, both the medieval and CIA state-of-the-art variety.

The next days weren't as bad; there were even some pleasant moments. Was the landscape beautiful? I suppose it might have been, but after that first night when I'd shed most of my human qualities, food, drink and shelter were the only things that retained significance. I felt something akin to pleasure when catching, cooking and consuming the walleyes, and I particularly enjoyed Bill's tradition of awarding everyone a shot of peppermint schnapps after they caught a fish. It made me fight harder on the reel and it burned going down.

## A Wild Search for Self
By Rachel Garwin

I didn't expect my most humbling moment to come at the hands of a resentful, sullen, homesick, self-isolating 15-year-old. Let's call him Jon. But there I sat, feeling the penetrating heat of his words as they burned in my mind. The comments from my student now – compared to what he'd been saying over the previous three weeks – testified to the transformative power of Minnesota's Boundary Waters Canoe Area, which we had just left. As I listened, I thought back to the Jon who had showed up 20 days earlier.

My co-leader and I welcomed the teenagers and made sure their long underwear was warm enough, that they had enough socks, and that their packs contained absolutely no cotton. Jon was mostly silent; he offered one-word answers or none at all. I wondered whether his lack of response meant shyness or something worse.

At dinner that night, Jon clarified his attitude. My co-leader asked our students to share why they had decided to venture into the BWCA. As his fellow students opened up, Jon sat with his face covered by his stretchy orange bandana-like neck gaiter. I could only see his eyes, making it impossible to read his facial expressions. Finally, it was his turn. "I was forced to come. It was either this or summer school," he resentfully told the group. He added that he couldn't last the full three weeks in the wilderness, that it would be too hard. When a fellow student suggested that he might learn something about himself if he stuck with the experience, Jon simply shrugged him off.

We pushed off from the Moose Lake landing and entered the

BWCA. Over the next few days, our students fell into the swing of backcountry life. We woke early. They collected firewood. They honed their paddle strokes. Portages forced the students to help each other lift packs and trade off carrying canoes on their shoulders. We expected Jon to contribute, and bit by bit, he began doing so.

Jon's first breakthrough occurred on the fourth day. We awoke in a cramped, overgrown campsite. Space was limited, and so we had wedged the canoes in questionable places when putting them to bed the previous night. As a result, they were hard as hell to get down to the water in the morning. Two other students struggled to work a 75- pound boat through closely growing balsam firs, and Jon spontaneously walked over to help them. Until then, group members needed to ask him to lend a hand before he would act. Jon was on his way.

We traveled through the misty, drizzly day until we reached the slate-gray depths of Knife Lake. Stymied multiple times the previous day by occupied campsites, we chose the first we found. We set about our now-familiar tasks: collecting fire- wood, building a wet fire, setting up tents and a tarp.

After dinner, I led a ceremony asking each student to com- mit to the group and to the expedition. Most of them set nice, though vague, goals. "I'll carry more weight," one said. Another promised continued "positive mental attitude." When it was Jon's turn, he lowered his bandana/gaiter – he had worn it con- tinuously – and committed to "trying to be less of a dick." I was floored. Very promising, indeed.

A week and a half later, Jon had transformed completely. He developed into a diligent navigator and unfailingly directed his group toward the correct portage landings. The group recog- nized and appreciated him for his physical strength. Jon was twice the size of the smallest student, who initially could barely pick up a 40-pound pack without falling over. Jon helped other students lift their packs at portages, and he often was the one to backtrack for the last bag. He carried more gear and food than many of the other students.

Two and a half weeks after the resentful and self-isolating Jon had arrived, a laughing, confident, and compassionate Jon had taken his place. He wore his bandana/gaiter only to avoid mosquitoes, not his group mates. He smiled and cracked jokes with his peers. Jon finally felt included, and he fully participated in the group culture.

By journey's end, Jon was changed person, one who felt confident enough to try out for his high school's football team despite a previous statement that he never would play football again. I asked Jon what he was most proud of, a standard question for these final conversations. "I'm stronger than everyone else. People relied on me," he said. Then he added, "I'm not as selfish as when I came. I wanted the group to have the best." Pride infused his voice, where there was none before. The inward-focused, resentful young person had changed into a truly loyal, caring member of the group. He put others' needs above his own. Perhaps most importantly, he felt proud not only that he was strong, but his strength was integral to group success. The group relied on him, and that reliance fueled his feeling of inclusion and self-worth. Jon recognized his conversations with others as one of the things that sustained him during the challenging times. He saw his own value and worth reflected in others' appreciation for his actions. After all, in order to believe you can help someone else, you must first believe you have something to offer.

Wilderness had again worked its magic.

## Rapping To Silence
By Joel Spoonheim

Bursting off the bus, Taisha and her friends brought a blast of noise, laughter and bombastic rap to the silence of our deep-woods parking lot. This group was a hodgepodge from a tough neighborhood, thrown together by an afterschool program and treated to a week at camp.

After piling them and their gear into a 12-person canoe, we took the group to the island on which they'd sleep before venturing out. From our camper cabin, people all over Seagull Lake heard the kids' utter dismay as we confiscated each MP3 player, hair product and deodorant. Angrily, Taisha improvised a profanity-laced rap about the oppression of white men, which prompted even her girlfriends to say, "Yo, you can't say that, T."

We set out the next morning to experience many firsts: zigzagging across the lake as kids explored paddling for the first time. First time setting up a tent. First time gathering wood for a fire. First time eating trail food. First time sitting on an open latrine while swatting mosquitoes.

Taisha was clearly the ringleader of the group. She'd have the other kids rapping every waking moment. Rap, never my favorite genre, was a particularly harsh intruder in a place that I cherished as a quiet, sacred sanctuary. On day three, late in the morning after a brief paddling break, I assigned her to the front of my canoe, hoping that being partnered with me would quiet her.

Nope. My aluminum canoe turned out to be a serviceable beatbox. After nicely asking her to keep paddling a few times, I finally lost my cool. Half-yelling, I pleaded, "Taisha, can't you please be quiet? What's wrong with quiet?"

She yelled back at me, voice full of defiance, "I hate quiet. In my neighborhood, it only gets this quiet after somebody gets shot."

On the last night, we told the kids they had to be self-sufficient: set up the tents, cook the food, everything. I left the camp to go fishing; I was just around the corner but within earshot. I forced myself to stay away. I was not looking forward to what I was sure I'd find upon my return: disorder, disarray and defiance.

After an hour or so, I half-heartedly headed back to the campsite, bracing myself for complaints and conflict. To my surprise, I was greeted by the glorious scene of smoke rising – one kid was stoking the fire while another stirred the pot. A slack but upright tent stood proudly nearby. There was no blood, no fighting, just a group of kids huddled around a fire, proudly welcoming me back. Of course, Taisha immediately began a rap about the camp guide who got skunked at the fishing hole, not realizing that my broad smile was evidence of an even greater bounty. Indeed, my heart was filled with affection and hope for this group of noisy kids who challenged me to help change their world to be one that welcomed quiet.

# *Where 0°F Feels Like Summer*
By Rachel Garwin

For the first time in days, I watched solid water melt into liquid in the open air. I'd witnessed only the reverse process since we'd started mushing three days before. Fire roared in front of me, fueled by pieces of split jackpine and black spruce. The night was finally warm enough to liberate us from the canvas-wall tent, and we cooked and ate beneath the dark sky. Flakes fell steadily and melted where they landed on my legs, enough to dampen the windproof nylon above my knees. I marveled at the warm night. The thermometer read 3°F.

Our snowy night on Thomas Lake was the first time air temperature had broken zero during our expedition. We'd experienced a 30-degree swing from that very morning, when the thermometer registered -27°F. Those are a very important 30 degrees.

What does it mean to live outside for consecutive days between zero and -35°F? Everything is more difficult at 35 degrees below zero. The unavoidable moments when one exposes skin to take care of bodily needs must be executed purposefully: first remove just one big mitten, next the outer pants come down, then insulating pants, quick pee, insulating pants back up, outer pants back up, big mitten back on, hand never leaving its liner glove. Waking up requires a deliberate sequence involving donning liner gloves, eating a calorie-rich snack, drinking water, pulling on bottom layers, and putting on a headlamp, all before un-cinching the hoods of your two sleeping bags. Even fully dressed, packing up camp includes jogging in place frequently to pump heat to hands and feet. Standing still only gets you colder.

Steam freezes on the cooking tripod chains only a foot above where it had just escaped pots of boiling water. The lakes boom as ice forms. Every protruding hair frosts within seconds. Eyelashes, eyebrows, and nose hairs all freeze, sometimes uncomfortably. Damp articles of clothing freeze solid or frost-over when removed from body heat. It is too cold for snow to fall.

On our last morning, I woke in the dark to a warning that it was 20 below. "Put on your down parkas first thing. It's really cold." The hood of my inner bag was lined with frost, and my nose hairs were frozen together.

# PINE DUFF

## You Are Invited: A 1927 Pro-Development Junket to the Lake Country

In early September, 1927, the "Backus-Brooks Special" departed Minneapolis for points north. This luxury rail junket was a marketing gimmick to wine and dine publishers, printers and other customers of Edward W. Backus and William F. Brooks, owners of the Backus-Brooks Company. Backus was a powerful turn-of-the-century industrialist. He'd earned a fortune as a lumber baron. He owned multiple timber and paper mills, and a hydro-electric dam. Starting in the mid-1920s, he was the visionary behind a radical plan to build seven dams in what is now the Boundary Waters Canoe Area. The dams would have changed the area forever, dramatically raising water levels and spurring additional development in the sparsely populated region. In the process, Backus' fortune would grow exponentially.

He had much going in his favor. At the time, the U.S. was giddy with the gains of a wild bull stock market (which would crash two years later with the start of the Great Depression). Pro-business sentiment reigned. "Environmentalism" was a marginal philosophy, with few adherents, minimal organization, and little power to stop a project that promised many jobs and big profits.

Nonetheless, a small group led by Ernest Oberholtzer organized resistance to Backus' plan. In time, their vision prevailed, preserving the beautiful wilderness region along the Minnesota-Canada border ... what is now the BWCA and Quetico.

To give a sense of what Oberholtzer and friends were up against, below are excerpts from the invitation to the Brooks-Backus junket, delivered in a specially designed cloth pouch.

# BACKUS-BROOKS SPECIAL
## *Minnesota & Ontario Paper Company Outing Party*
### Sept. 5-14, 1927
#### Leaving Minneapolis 7 p.m. Sept. 5, 1927

### Itinerary and General Program

The guests of the Company will include its newsprint paper customers – publishers located throughout the Middle West – and the officials of all the railway systems radiating from the Twin Cities and from Winnipeg.

The Backus-Brooks Special train, consisting of Pullman sleepers, dining cars and railway official business cars, will convey the party during the entire trip.

Guests are requested to arrive in Minneapolis on Monday, Sept. 5. The privileges of the Minikahda Club will be extended to those who wish to play golf during the day and those gentlemen should bring their own sticks with them. Others can spend the day calling on friends or acquaintances in Minneapolis, or in touring the boulevards, which are numerous and beautiful.

### Tuesday September 6th

**7:00 a.m.** Arrive International Falls. Breakfast will be served on the train. Inspect the Company's mills (in Fort Francis Ontario).

**2:00 p.m.** Dutch Luncheon will be served by the citizens of Fort Francis.

**4:00 p.m.** Leave Fort Francis over the Canadian National Railways for the Canadian Twin Cities – Fort William and Port Arthur. En route a stop will be made at Sturgeon Falls to inspect the Company's new hydro-electric power plan. Time will not permit visiting the two new Hydro-Electronic power plants at Calm Lake and Moose Lake.

### Rainey Lake (sic)

The area of Rainey Lake is 300 square miles in which there are 3,000 islands. Immediately above the beautiful body of water is the Namakan chain of Lakes, having an area of 120 square miles.

**THURSDAY, SEPT. 8**

**12:00 P.M.** Lunch on the train.

**1:00 P.M.** Off for the fishing grounds.

**3:00 P.M.** Fishing in productive waters for black bass and lake trout. We suggest that those who have fishing tackle bring it with them. Any who prefers fishing for Muskalonge (sic) will be provided the opportunity.

**7:00 P.M.** Barbecue. The night will be spent on the beach in tents.

The Lake of Woods has grown famous as a fishing region. The angler has not any difficulty in finding the smallmouth black bass, pickerel, great northern pike, and muskalonge within a radius from three to twenty miles from Kenora. Salmon and lake trout are generally found beyond this area.

**FRIDAY, SEPTEMBER 9TH**

Breakfast on Beach

Fishing all day

**1:00 P.M.** Luncheon

**5:00 P.M.** Buffet lunch.

**7:00 P.M.** Barbecue and Sturgeon Dinner. Another night in tents.

A splendid nine-hole course of 2,725 yards is situated about one mile from the Kenora Post Office, and is easily accessible by land or water. It is considered an exceedingly sporty course; the tees and greens being elevated command excellent views of the surrounding country and lake.

# BWCA QUIZ #4

**1.)**  Prior to the 1920s and '30s, what were the two dominant fish species in BWCA lakes?

**2.)**  In 1971, these were introduced into the BWCA; by 1975 BWCA regulations made use of them mandatory. What are they?

**3.)**  What was the "High Wine" drink treasured by the voyageurs?

**4.)**  In 1968, all BWCA visitors were issued a permit plus one other item. What was that item?

**5.)**  How many calories would a 150-pound person burn canoeing for one hour, at a speed of four miles per hour?

### BWCA Quiz #4 – Answers

1.)  Lake Trout and Northern Pike. Walleyes were found in only a few lakes. Bass (largemouth and smallmouth) and crappies had not yet been planted into lakes in large numbers.

2.)  Designated campsites. Today, the BWCA has about 2,200 designated campsites (marked on maps, each site features installed steel fire grates and a box latrine).

3.)  "High Wine" was a high-proof liquor, a twice-distilled, 160-proof rum (about 80 percent alcohol content). It was often diluted before measured servings were doled out to voyageurs.

4.)  In 1968, BWCA users were "requested" to burn all burnable garbage and papers, and to carry out all non-burnable waste. When travel permits were issued, BWCA visitors were given a garbage bag, to encourage them to carry out non-burnable waste (bottles and cans).

5.)  The answer depends on which calorie calculator you use, but most estimates range from about 500 calories to slightly over 600 calories.

# Canoe Country Quotations

by Francis L. Jaques

*Published in 1931, in* The Journal of The American Museum of Natural History.

Artist Francis Lee Jaques (1887-1969) was a staff artist at the museum. Jaques also illustrated books by canoe country author Sigurd Olson. The American Museum of Natural History in New York City, founded in 1869, is one of the world's preeminent scientific and cultural institutions. The quotes below are reprinted with permission from a 1931 essay titled "Canoe Country," published by the American Museum of Natural History.

To learn more about the Museum, or to become a member, visit: http://www.amnh.org/

"Over these same portages, landing on the very rocks used today, the hardy men of the Northwest Company maintained, by their canoes, the only communication with posts as far west as Saskatchewan and the Yellowstone, and explored the Mackenzie and Frazer Rivers."

"Loons: Their weird calls, once heard in the Northern Wilderness, can never be forgotten."

"...no man will ever know how many lakes it (the Quetico-Superior Area) contains until it is mapped by airplane."

"The entire region is of ancient granite, heavily scored in several directions by the former ice cap, resulting in numerous depressions filled with deep, cool lakes of clear water. Lakes away from the main watercourses sometimes are unbelievably clear, so that one has the weird impression that one's canoe is floating through the air."

"...the region is only useful as a wilderness area – a real museum of the past, a 'university of the wilderness.'"

"Weather, largely overlooked in the city, becomes of vital importance. The direction and velocity of the wind determine the route you take, or whether you travel at all. You scan the map anxiously for long stretches of water, and try to avoid them. You come to feel a relationship between cloud shadows and gusts of wind. You treasure the rare days when the water is like glass, showing the inverted image of the sky and the lakes seem full to overflowing – truly a setting to inspire the lover of the outdoors."

"It is not pleasant to say that this wilderness is threatened. Commercial interests have proposed ... to raise the water (level) varying amounts from five to eighty-two feet with the resulting destruction of the present shorelines, and a rise and fall of water which leaves an encircling fringe of dead trees... A determined group of men, represented by the Quetico-Superior Council, is working against odds to preserve this area in its original state."